RACISM
THE INEVITABLE IN AMERICA

EDWARD FAISON, JR.

RACISM, THE INEVITABLE IN AMERICA
Copyright © 2022 by Edward Faison, Jr.

All rights reserved. No part of this publication may be reproduced, distributed, or transmitted in any form or by any means, including photocopying, recording, or other electronic or mechanical methods, without the prior written permission of the publisher or author, except in the case of brief quotations embodied in critical reviews and certain other noncommercial uses permitted by copyright law.

Although every precaution has been taken to verify the accuracy of the information contained herein, the author and publisher assume no responsibility for any errors or omissions. No liability is assumed for damages that may result from the use of information contained within.

Library of Congress Control Number: 2021906496
ISBN-13:   Paperback: 978-1-64749-426-1
           E-pub: 978-1-64749-427-8

Printed in the United States of America

GoTo Publish

GoToPublish LLC
1-888-337-1724
www.gotopublish.com
info@gotopublish.com

Contents

Chapter1. The Way I See It 1
Chapter2. Slavery from Africa 5
Chapter3. Slavery in America 9
Chapter4. The Civil War 15
Chapter5. The Ku Klux Klan 21
Chapter6. Freedom 25
Chapter7. The Reconstruction Period 27
Chapter8. Politics and Voting Rights 31
Chapter9. Sharecropping 37
Chapter10. Migration from the South 39
Chapter11. World War I 45
Chapter12. Consistent Racism and Violence 51
Chapter13. How I Learned about Racism 55
Chapter14. My Introduction to Fear and Violence 57
Chapter15. My Introduction to Segregation 61
Chapter16. More Segregation 63
Chapter17. Segregation within the Black Race 65
Chapter18. The White Woman as a Cause of Racism in
America 67
Chapter19. Exploitation 69
Chapter20. World War II 71
Chapter21. The Woodyard 77
Chapter22. Mother's Job 81
Chapter23. Dislike of My Own Hair 85
Chapter24. Polarization of the Races 89
Chapter25. Teenage Memories 93
Chapter26. North Carolina College for Negroes 107
Chapter27. Me and Uncle Sam 111
Chapter28. The Sixties 131

Chapter 29. Separate but Equal 133
Chapter 30. More on Integration 135
Chapter 31. Racism on the Job 137
Chapter 32. Malcolm X—a Great Antiracist of His Day 155
Chapter 33. The March on Washington 161
Chapter 34. The 1968 Riots in D.C. 163
Chapter 35. How a Few Blacks Got Rich 169
Chapter 36. Muhammad Ali 175
Chapter 37. The Last Protest 177
Chapter 38. Racism, the Inevitable in America 181

Appendix: Poems and Articles by Edward Faison, Jr.

Y'all C'mon Home and Buy Freedom 196
A Message to African-Americans 199
Blacks' Prayer for Thanksgiving 204
Should African-Americans Dislike Moammar
Khadafy? 206
About Martin Luther King, Jr.'s Birthday 210
I Still Like Jesse Jackson, But 212
Dreaming of a Black Christmas 215
Young, Gifted, and Black 217

Chapter 1
The Way I See It

In the beginning, when Africa was black and everybody in a tribe looked the same, there was no racism. When all tribal members were basically the same color and all of their hair was kinky, dark skin posed no problem and kinky hair was the standard. Tribal members paid special attention to their hair and in many cases were identified by it. They wore exotic styles decorated with gold and precious stones. These black men, women, and children were truly brilliant and beautiful.

Africans were and still are a people of tradition. They did the same thing, approximately the same time, year in and year out. No one dared defy their elders and do something different. Why would they anyway, when the way they were doing things had worked for thousands and thousands of years?

The only problem with doing the same thing year in and year out is that nothing new occurs. So doing the same thing worked against these blacks when the enemy came.

Traditionally, Africans were peaceful and peaceable people. They had no violent weapons intended primarily for killing human beings. Their weapons were mainly used for hunting and for sport. They had no guns and explosive weapons, because they had no need for such weapons. Though they were excellent craftsmen and smiths, they saw no need for a weapon to be used almost exclusively for killing people.

Africans exhibited their strength in many ways; no examples of which were concerned with how many human beings they could kill. When they fought wars, they were more about conquering than killing. Unlike the white man, the blacks did not destroy as they conquered. When Africans claimed victory over a country, some of the people they conquered were enslaved, but not forever. Slavery among Africans was humane and for a definite period of time. Moreover, the enslaved people could keep their names and identities. Their culture was respected, and they were allowed to keep their family ties. A slave could work his way out of bondage. In many cases, if a slave during that time desired to become a respected member of the African family for whom he or she toiled, the slave could do so and remain with them the rest of their lives if he chose to do so.

Degrading their enemy was not the sole purpose for fighting a war according to African culture. War was more like a game rather than being based on enjoying killing, conquering, and taking land.

A good example of how slavery was a way of life at that time can be found in the Bible (Genesis 37:28). According to the story, Joseph's brothers supposedly sold him into slavery in Africa for little or nothing (twenty pieces of silver). A good example of how slaves were treated at that time was illustrated in the same book. According to the story, when the brothers came to Egypt for grain, it was Joseph, the so-called slave, who was passing out the grain and who invited them in to relax and enjoy his place of abode. Though he was supposedly a slave, he was apparently at ease and was obviously being treated like a human being. He had proudly held onto his identity and did not appear to be a threat to run away. In fact, according to the story he did not seem anxious to return home with his brothers.

When the white man showed up in Africa, there was plenty of gold for everyone. The Africans' attitude toward gold was like the Indians' attitude toward land when the white man first came to America. The Indians felt there was plenty for everyone. They had no way of knowing about the greed of the white man.

When the white man learned of the Africans' fascination with bright colored cloth and trinkets, they were practically overcome with greed. Here again, the Africans attitude was, "You want gold and/or slaves for cloth and trinkets, fine." They knew gold was plentiful, and they felt quite sure that the slaves they sold to the white men would be treated the way slaves were traditionally treated by Africans.

The white men wasted no time setting up trading posts, and swapping something for nothing was right down their alley. But being greedy as they were, they wanted "the whole hog."

Shortly after their invasion of Africa, the white man introduced Africans to guns and explosives. The white men had but to kill a few Africans with guns for the entire tribe to succumb before them in fear. Not having seen such devastating weapons before, the Africans would turn in fear and run for their lives. The white predators would take all they desired, burn what was left, and move on.

Chapter 2
Slavery from Africa

While white men were discovering gold and slaves in Africa, there were white men in a so-called new land, America, who were in need of some workers to toil in their cotton and tobacco fields. They had tried enslaving other white men as they were brought to America for various reasons, but this did not work because many of these white men were lazy. Their backs were weak and they could not deal with the hot sun of the South, which beamed down for long hours. Besides that, the slave owners found themselves in court too often, defending their right to hold a white man in slavery. When a white slave ran away, he could easily mix into the population and escape.

The white men tried enslaving the Indians, and this too was virtually impossible. First of all, the Indians knew the terrain better than their enslavers and were used to traveling through the bushes and along the rivers. Many Indians also had weak backs and were worshippers of the land and their environment and did not believe in desecrating the land as the white man did. (The Indians called the white men "Desecrators of Land.")

The Africans made perfect slaves in America for a number of reasons. The climate in the South was much like the climate in Africa; therefore, the Africans could readily deal with the hot sun. They were good farmers in Africa so they would not have to be taught how to farm. They had strong backs, were resourceful, and could build and repair things. Africans were innovative and skillful, exactly what was needed in this so-called newly discovered land. Many were easily identifiable because their complexion was jet black. They would be a long ways from home and the only people with a black complexion in America. White men would have total jurisdiction over the blacks, and they would have no right in court. In fact, they would be treated more like animals than human beings.

White men immediately began to set up slave-holding camps all along the coasts of Africa. Other Africans were placed in charge of the camps. Buying, selling, and trading human beings became big business from the shores of Africa to the shores of America. White men supplied the guns to the Africans who captured other Africans and brought them to the slave-holding camps. It was greed on the part of the African and white men that kept such an unsavory and inhumane market in operation. It was virtually impossible for other Africans to stop the whites because those employed by the white man had the fire power. They gave this power to greedy Africans along with a few material things, and this made the whites stronger and more powerful than African kings and their armies.

In the holding camps, Africans who rebelled were dealt with in various ways. They were threatened, separated from their families, and sometimes beaten. They were fed and kept healthy only so they would bring a good price at the market. If a captive continued to refuse to succumb or conform, he or she was publicly tortured to death and thrown overboard. This supposedly would serve notice to others who might be thinking of rebelling.

The slave ships were carefully navigated up to the gates of the slave-holding camps. Slaves were marched onto the ships like cattle, shackled hand and feet to each other. They were packed in on several tiers of the ships as close together as they could be packed. The more slaves loaded, the more money in the ship captain's pocket. Once the voyage had begun, the slaves would be brought up to the top deck at least once a day to be hosed down because many of the slaves would become seasick and vomit or be sick with loose bowels. Of course their hair would be wooly, matted, and sometimes lice-ridden.

The ship hands would be careful never to unlock the shackles because some of the slaves were eager to rebel. Some would jump overboard rather than be taken away to a strange land. Some chose to commit suicide any way they could the first chance they got. There were still others whom the captain of the ship would have to kill on the spot because they refused to succumb to being enslaved by another human being. Only the strong survived or chose to survive. On many ships, nine out of ten slaves did not make it.

Africans were proud people, free from fear, hunger, and racism. They were taken away from their homeland, never to return. They also left behind in Africa many sad families who were suddenly without their children, never to know where they had been taken or to hear from them again.

The white man burned, destroyed, and raped the continent of Africa. They took a hundred million of the strongest men, women, and children from their land. They stole everything of value from Africa and labeled it the Dark Continent. They refused to tell the truth about the advanced civilization the Africans were enjoying before they destroyed it. Instead, they portrayed the Africans as savages, running around in the jungles with bones through their noses. They told wild tales about uncivilized black people who ate each other (cannibals). All this marked the beginning of what was later known as the peculiar institution of slavery in America.

Chapter 3
Slavery in America

The Spaniards, who were masters at enslaving human beings, warned the Americans not to treat the African slave as a human being. This was the beginning of racism toward the Africans in America (social discrimination). The Spaniards strongly recommended that the slaves be dropped off at the West Indies Islands and be trained to be good, obedient slaves in America. These slaves' training camps were run by the Spaniards, and that is why most of the black inhabitants who remain on the islands today speak Spanish. Some slaves who had already learned to speak English and were known to be loyal were also used to train new slaves on the islands. They told them about America and why they should not resist being enslaved there. The slaves were treated like horses being brought to a ranch to be broken. Here again, some rebelled and had to be killed. Others ran away to the swamps or jungles, while still others committed suicide. The majority of them conformed to slavery and were brought to America to be auctioned off to the highest bidder.

Being bought and sold like cattle was a very traumatic experience for a group of people who had been used to peace and harmony. They could not believe another man could be so inconsiderate of another human being. Africans were inherently people who felt trust and love for their fellowmen. As a matter of fact, this is one reason they found themselves in a distant land, far away from home, in an unknown country. They were brought to this foreign land and told not to even look toward Africa again. They were not allowed to venture from the immediate area unless they had permission from their master. They were taught to be totally dependent on the master. African slaves did not know the English language, but they were not allowed to speak in their native tongues. Africans in America had no country, no name, and no identity. A human being in a strange land with no identity was hardly a threat to anyone.

The African slaves were seldom allowed to congregate at any time except for work. Whispering was against the rules; standing taller than the master, talking back to the master were crimes punished by any means the master saw fit. Any white man could challenge any slave about anything without rebuttal. This was institutionalized racism. Slaves were taught to be class conscious and to think of themselves as second-class, subhuman beings.

In many cases, slaves were treated more like animals than humans. They were fed mush in troughs on many plantations, and they ate with their hands. They slept on the ground or on improvised beds made from straw or hay. The same was true of housing. Many found housing in the barn with the animals. Some slaves received shoes at the beginning of the summer and at Christmastime. Others went barefoot the year round. Food consisted of scraps that the master didn't want, such as pigs' feet, tails, ears, innards (chitterlings), and neckbones, cornbread, and beans. Most of the clothes were hand-me-downs from the "Big House."

Slaves were four hundred years without a comb that would accommodate their hair. In Africa, combs were made for the purpose of combing kinky hair. Combs used by Europeans were not suitable for combing Africans' hair. The Africans' hair became a problem the moment they were placed on the slave ships and continued to be a problem throughout the time they were enslaved. Their hair quickly became unkempt, dirty, wooly, and lousy. There were no combs, brushes, shampoo, or hair oil for the slaves' hair. They were made to be extremely sensitive about their hair and were taught to keep their distance from white people because of the lice and other bugs that made a home in the blacks' heads. White women were especially protected from the slaves and their lousy heads. Many of the slaves put axle grease on their hair and heads in an attempt to kill the lice and thus stop the itching. Whenever possible, they would cut their hair with the shears used to cut the horses' tails and manes. Ringworm and other scalp diseases were common among slaves. This of course made the slaves hate their own hair and wish it would not grow. Worse than that. it encouraged them to admire their masters' hair and thus the theory of "straight hair being good hair" was derived.

Seeing themselves as black, repugnant, kinky-headed, and unwanted was a new experience for these African people. It was also a rude awakening because black skin and kinky hair were the worst things one could have in America. African slaves began wishing they were white like their enslavers. Wishing you are someone else might mean that you hate being yourself. Worst yet, the slaves accepting the home of their enslaver and wanting to look like them meant they were truly enslaved in every way.

Big, strong male African slaves brought the most money at the slave auction houses. Strong slave women that were still of child-bearing age also brought a good price. The latter were a good buy because they could cook, bear children, and in many cases control the other slaves. The slave owners and their friends could also enjoy the women sexually at will. A slave woman was sometimes allowed to go free if she had at least ten children. A big, strong slave man and a strong slave woman were sometimes put together and forced to breed like animals. Some slave women would kill their babies in their wombs before they were born rather than have them born into slavery. The slave owner could rape any of the slave women if and when he chose to. In fact, some would make it known that a certain slave woman belonged to them and none of the male slaves would dare approach her sexually. Though many of these chosen women objected to such an arrangement, they often had children by the white master and these children would more than likely receive preferential treatment. Invariably, the baby, like the white master, was light-skinned. At least in most cases, the baby was lighter than his or her shiny black sisters and brothers from Africa. Many light-skinned slaves were treated differently by the slave owners because they were part of their masters flesh and blood. For the most part, this new kind of slave worked in or around the house. Being labeled a "house nigger" made him or her the envy of his peers. Now you have human beings who not only wish they had hair like their masters, but also wished they had light skin and straight hair like the "house nigger." The light-skinned slave also received respect and different treatment from other slaves. They were expected to keep the master informed as to what was happening among the other slaves; thus the owner had a self-made surveillance system at his disposal. For this reason the "house niggers" were not trusted by the "field niggers." This definitely caused dissension among the slaves. This is also the origin of certain variants of racism within the African-American people. Social discrimination and racial discrimination became a factor among the slaves for the first time.

Slave trading continued to be prosperous for many, many years. Cotton and tobacco was the chief crops down south, and the more slaves a farmer owned the more money he could make. He could get free labor on his own land, and whenever possible he would hire his slaves out to other landowners for additional profits. The more slaves a man owned, the greater his say was among his peers. In some states, slaves outnumbered the white residents. This was something that had to be reckoned with, especially after the insurrection staged by Nat Turner in Virginia.

Though slaves continued to rebel for many years while being brought from Africa to America, opposition to slavery by freed men and slaves slowly subsided as the years passed. New slaves that might have rebelled were confronted by slaves that had given up fighting and trying to return to Africa. They would insist that a new slave should be obedient. The slave owner would use group pressure, and if the old slaves allowed a new or old slave to escape, the master would punish all of the slaves. When the runaway slave was caught, the other slaves would be forced to watch while the cruel punishment was inflicted. Most of the time the punishment would consist of lashing, snatching out the runaway's tongue, or even hanging him.

Opposition to slavery also declined because many slaves after a few years were born into slavery and of course knew nothing of Africa. Their parents and other slaves were afraid to talk about Africa, so there was no way for the children to hear about it. This way, children who were born into slavery knew nothing of African culture and their African heritage. Slaves were taught to love America, the home of their enslavers.

When a slave ran away, most of the time he had no idea where he was running to. Throughout their lives, most slaves had no idea where they were except for the fact that they were in America. They went from one field to another or from one farm to another. There was mostly wilderness and undeveloped land in the southern states. There were no freeways to freedom. Anyway, escaping to somewhere else was seldom attempted because there were too many white men to answer to along the road to so-called freedom.

Another method used by the slave masters to keep the slaves docile was giving them alcohol. When all of the work ended on Saturday evening, slaves were allowed to get drunk and "whoop it up." Singing, dancing, and clowning were expected and encouraged. A drunk slave would not be a threat to run away. A slave who chose to remain quiet and sober was suspected as a potential troublemaker. Other slaves would be designated to watch quiet slaves. Drunken brawls, fun, and games went on throughout the weekend. Slave owners thought a happy slave was a contented slave and as long as he was making noise, he was easy to keep up with.

Finally, opposition to slavery diminished among the slaves because they were allowed to be Christians. Christianity was used by the slave owners to keep their slaves meek and humble. Slaves were taught that it was a sin to lie, cheat, steal, or run away. Good slaves did not oppose the slave master, and most of all, Christianity kept the slaves busy on Sunday.

Chapter 4
The Civil War

The slaves proved to be a problem during the War between the States. The problems stemmed from the fact that many slaves were escaping from the South and joining the Union Army. It was a pleasure for most of them to fight a war against the people of the South who had enslaved them for so many years. Most of all, slaves were promised freedom by the Union once the war was over. The war was being won handily by the Union, partially because of the slaves who defected to their side. Following is the story of one such slave:

> First Sgt. Decatur Dorsey, a member of Company B, 39th Regiment of the U.S. Colored Troop, earned the nation's highest military honor for saving the colors and rallying the troops at the battle of Petersburg, Va., in 1864. He was one of 186,000 slaves who fought in the Union Army and one of the 56 blacks among the 2,357 servicemen awarded the Medal of Honor since 1863. Sgt. Dorsey, once a Maryland slave, rode ahead of his troops into a hail of enemy fire on July 30, 1864, at Petersburg and planted the flag on Confederate territory. The black troops had been sent in after an assault by a white company failed. But when Union troops saw the flag, they forged ahead only to be driven back again. Dorsey carried the flag in retreat and rallied his men to a new assault. Later a Union commander ordered a full retreat, but the black

brigade's casualty list of 1,324 was the longest of any of the three attacking divisions.

As you know, not all blacks were ardent Union supporters. A small minority favored the South and were outspoken Confederate sympathizers. Many of them were arrested and jailed. Blacks were so brainwashed that they could not come together even when their freedom would be the end result.

Being lazy, some southern white men sent one or two slaves to fight on their behalf. This often proved to be a mistake because some of the slave warriors escaped to the Union Army and took their weapons with them. Something had to be done because slavery was the backbone of the South. Southerners pleaded with President Abraham Lincoln to do something. President Lincoln unwillingly signed the Emancipation Proclamation in February 1863.

THE EMANCIPATION PROCLAMATION (1863)

By the President of the United States of America:
A Proclamation

Whereas on the 22nd day of September, A.O. 1863, all persons held as slaves within any State or designated part of a State the people whereof shall then be in rebellion against the United States shall be then, thenceforward, and forever free; and the executive government of the United States, including the military and naval authority thereof, will recognize and maintain the freedom of such persons, or any of them, in any efforts they may make for their actual freedom.

"That the executive will on the 1st day of January aforesaid, by proclamation, designate the States and parts of States, if any, in which the people thereof, respectively, shall then be in rebellion against the United States; and the fact that any State or the people thereof shall on that day be in good faith represented in the Congress of the United States by members chosen thereto at elect ions wherein a majority of the qualified voters of such States shall have participated shall, in the absence of strong countervailing testimony, be deemed conclusive evidence that such State and the people thereof are not then in rebellion against the United States."

Now, therefore, I, Abraham Lincoln, President of the United States, by virtue of the power in me vested as Commander-in-Chief of the Army and Navy of the United States in time of actual armed rebellion against the authority and government of the United States, and as a fit and necessary war measure for suppressing said rebellion, do, on this 1st day of January, A.O. 1863, and in accordance with my purpose so to do, publicly proclaim for the full period of one hundred days from the first day above mentioned, order and designate as the States and parts of States wherein the people thereof, respectively, are this day in rebellion against the United States the following, to wit:

Arkansas, Texas, Louisiana (except the parishes of St. Bernard, Plaquemines, Jefferson, St. John, St. Charles, St. James, Ascension, Assumption,

Terrebonne, Lafourche, St. Mary, St. Martin and Orleans, including the city of New Orleans), Mississippi, Alabama, Florida, Georgia, South Carolina, North Carolina, and Virginia (except the forty eight counties designated as West Virginia, and also the counties of Berkeley, Accomack, North Hampton, Elizabeth City, York, Princess Anne, and Norfolk, including the cities of Norfolk and Portsmouth), and which excepted parts are for the present left precisely as if this proclamation were not issued.

And by virtue of the power and for the purpose aforesaid, I do order and declare that all persons held as slaves within said designated States and parts of States arc, and henceforward shall be, free; and that the Executive Government of the United States, including the military and naval authorities thereof, will recognize and maintain the freedom of said persons.

And I hereby enjoin upon the people so declared to be free to abstain from all violence, unless in necessary self-defense; and I recommend to them that, in all cases when allowed, they labor faithfully for reasonable wages.

And I further declare and make known that such persons of suitable condition will be received into the armed service of the United States to garrison forts, positions, stations, and other places, and to man vessels of all sorts in said service.

And upon this act, sincerely believed to be an act of justice, warranted by the Constitution upon military necessity, I invoke the considerate judgment of mankind and the gracious favor of Almighty God.

In testimony whereof, I have hereunto set my name, and caused the seal of the United States to be affixed.

Done at the City of Washington, this first day of January, in the year of our Lord one thousand eight hundred and sixty-three, and of the Independence of the United States the eighty-seventh.

By the President: Abraham Lincoln.

William H. Seward, Secretary of State

Slavery was abolished nationwide in 1865, when the Thirteenth Amendment to the U.S. Constitution was ratified:

Slavery Prohibited

Section 1. Neither slavery nor involuntary servitude, except as a punishment for crime whereof the party shall have been duly convicted, shall exist within the United States, or any place subject to their jurisdiction.

Section 2. Congress shall have power to enforce this article by appropriate legislation.

Chapter 5
The Ku Klux Klan

Ironically, the Ku Klux Klan was founded in the same year, 1865, that the Thirteenth Amendment was ratified.

Six ex-Confederate officers from Pulaski, Tennessee, supposedly decided to form a club in December 1865. They wanted the club to sound legitimate, like a regular college fraternity, so they decided to give it a Greek name and require a potential member to be initiated before he could become a full member. They came up with the name Ku Klux Klan because it seemed to have had a ring to it and meant "circle."

For the fun of it, these men decided to make robes and hoods out of bedsheets and pillowcases and wear them when they rode through the town of Pulaski at night. Even though they rode quietly, they soon learned that superstitious blacks were frightened by them. This was reason enough for white racists to join the Klan and enjoy frightening "niggers."

The Klan proved to be just what whites needed during the Reconstruction period to keep blacks from getting out of hand. They elected a superleader and called him the Imperial Wizard. They made terrorism the order of the day. They donned their costumes and frequently rode through the countryside looking for violence. Any black or white person who agreed with the nonracist policies could become a victim of this barbarous group. They lashed white teachers and set fires to buildings where blacks were being taught to read. Blacks who tried to do for themselves independently of the white man were beaten or killed. The Klan hanged, castrated, burned to death, and murdered blacks and dismembered their bodies like they were animals. This was happening all over the South, and the murderous Klan supposedly had the blessing of other whites who felt the South was being overtaken by African-Americans.

Soon the Klan became the law and a way of life in the South. They were the last word in the community and the courts. It was dangerous for another white to speak out against the Klan because Klansmen had no aversion to killing a white man or woman who was in sympathy with an African-American. They went virtually unchallenged and unpunished.

Even when the Klan did not have an active membership, more times than not a Klan mentality existed in white neighborhoods.

Again, it is ironic that the Ku Klux Klan was organized the same year blacks were supposed to have been freed. United Klans of America has flourished. With the Ku Klux Klan mentality being exhibited among whites all over America, it is reasonable to believe such a racist organization is not really necessary for racism to remain alive and active in this so-called democratic society.

Blacks had little or no recourse in white America when the former head of the Federal Bureau of Investigation labelled Martin Luther King, Jr. (Nobel Peace Prize winner) Americans' number one enemy while the Klan was bullying and murdering daily without objection from the top lawmen in the administration.

When the president of the United States is endorsed by a racist organization such as a Klan, blacks will have to band together to save themselves. For if the Klan and racism are ever to be stamped out in this country, it will have to be done from the top to the bottom. Pres. Lyndon B. Johnson probably made the greatest attempt to promote parity from the Oval Office, but failed to some extent in his attempt because racism was so prevalent in America.

Denying blacks their civil rights had become or always has been a way of life in America. Inasmuch as respect cannot be legislated, it would behoove blacks to pool their own minds and resources to possibly save themselves in a country where racism seems to be inevitable.

Chapter 6
Freedom

Slaves were freed with no money, no land, no jobs, and no rights, but they were free. "So what? You're free! So whatcha gonna do?" seemed to have been the attitude of the ex-slave master. Apparently he knew that four hundred years of total dependency could not be erased by the Thirteenth Amendment to the Constitution, especially when he was still in charge of many things of value in the United States. Slaves had been freed to make their way with nothing but the shirt on their backs.

Antiloitering laws were passed after the war because ex slaves were just loitering around in the streets. This gave the authorities the right to pick up ex-slaves in droves and hold them in jail until white men decided what to do with them. Most of the time, the former slaves' punishment was to be detained by a white fanner until his crops were harvested. Some ex-slaves were placed back with their old slave masters, where they were held illegally until they died.

Some slaves chose to remain where they were after they were "freed," because they knew they had nowhere to go and nothing to do. They knew they would still have to depend on their former masters for survival.

Nevertheless, some former slaves persevered. Many of the women were able to obtain employment because someone had to cook, wash, and iron for white people. Basically, they often worked for the scraps left from the meals, which they used to feed their families. The men picked up jobs here and there mostly on farms. Their biggest job was staying out of the way of white men. After the antiloitering laws were passed, ex-slaves would move as far away from white folks as they could to keep from being constantly abused and/or harassed. They would find obscure places out in the woods, build houses, and plant gardens for food. Their main sources of meat were chickens and hogs. This was the beginning of ex-slaves trying to help themselves. They would do fine until they were raided by white men who were determined not to let them make it on their own.

It is alleged that the governor of Mississippi at the time advised all white people who employed ex-slaves never to pay them any more than a week's worth of money. "That way," he said, "they will always be back to work on Monday morning."

Chapter 7
The Reconstruction Period

The Reconstruction period was all about reconstructing the South after the war. It had little or nothing to do with the ex-slaves except concerning what was to be done about these people whom white people used to own. According to the Thirteenth Amendment, the blacks were free, and southern white America had to find a place for them. The South was in total disarray, because the war had been devastating. Many of the so-called southern gentlemen found themselves without land, family, power, or slaves. In many ways, their plight was the same as or worse than that of the ex-slaves. As a matter of fact, they often found them selves competing with ex-slaves for jobs, land, and status.

The South was proving to be a terrible place for an ex-slave to live. They tried very hard to make it, in spite of the precarious situation they were in. The ex-slave immediately became expendable. "All da cotton ben picked; all da 'bacco dun ben cropped." There was little work left for them, and white men didn't intend to provide any for them. Jobs that the ex-slaves had performed while under slavery were being performed by white men. Many Frenchmen took over the cooking jobs, while some Italian men took over the barbering jobs. White men also took over the jobs of the ex-slave craftsmen and smiths. They continued to call themselves blacksmiths, but they were really "whitesmiths." Ex-slaves became helpers on jobs that were previously theirs exclusively. Other ex-slaves found themselves being considered un skilled workers on jobs where they previously had been considered skilled.

Male ex-slaves were systematically kept from the decent jobs now that they were supposed to be free, because the white man never wanted the black men to advance to the point where he would be admired and respected by white women. This was and still is the root of racism in America, especially after the black male was freed. This freedom, in essence, enslaved the male ex-slave and the white woman, leaving only the white man and the black woman free.

The southern white man was not prepared to compete with the male ex-slave for jobs, because the ex-slave was hungry. Africans had been good workers, strong and progressive. These traits did not change just because they were supposed to be free. If anything, the African-Americans became more aggressive, because they were anxious to make good with their so-called freedom. They had built America with no blueprints and for no money. They were ready to use their labor and skills for monetary gain. The ex-slave certainly did not fit the image of the shiftless and lazy bum that was being promulgated. Slave owners did not tolerate laziness during slavery, and a man does not become lazy just because a piece of paper has been signed.

The fact was, the white man had bred and created a big, strong, healthy "monster" that was out of his cage. The white man had been idle for four hundred years and had no real reason to use his back or his brain. He knew well who the shiftless and lazy one was and certainly did not wish to compete with him.

During the period shortly after slavery, ex-slaves tried hard to fit in. They were very conscious of their personal appearance because they had been nobody for so long that they had no idea who they should emulate and/or imitate. If you don't know who you are, then you are anyone and no one. This was the plight of the ex-slaves.

Unfortunately, the ex-slaves also could not resist the urge

to be like their ex-masters. They had been so brainwashed and isolated for so long they knew nothing else. They eagerly bought outfits like they had seen their former masters wear. They practiced talking like their former masters and were more sensitive than ever about their color and their hair.

Dark-complexioned African-Americans began courting and looking forward to marrying a light-skinned person, for their children's sake. When a light-skinned baby was born with straight hair, everyone called it cute and rejoiced. When a dark-skinned baby was born with kinky hair, it was not admired and no one rejoiced. African-Americans were beginning to hate themselves unless they resembled their formers masters. Later on, wigs, hair dyes, and bleaching creams became big sellers, because white men became aware of African-Americans' desire to look like them. They learned that they could make big money with these cosmetics, even though they knew all the bleaching cream and blond wigs in the world would not make the blacks white or give them the status of being white in America.

Four years after slavery had been abolished (1869), Mme. C. J. Walker invented the "straightening comb." She sold enough of the combs and stiff hair grease to become the first black female millionaire. She can also take the credit for much of the racism and confusion within the African-American race. African-Americans dreamed of having hair like their white enslavers, and the straightening comb and stiff grease were like a dream come true.

White women used rouge, powder, lipstick, and eye shadow to give them color and to cover up blood vessels that could be seen through their pale skin. African-Americans used cosmetics because white women used it. They didn't need any of it for color, and they certainly didn't need it to hide blood vessels.

African-Americans were enjoying equality like they never had before. Some white people became aware of the rapid change and immediately decided something had to be done about it. Some decided not to accept African-Americans in their unions, knowing that if they kept them from the job market, they would not have to worry about them making much progress. African Americans formed their own unions, but they were sabotaged by white people. They discouraged African-Americans from organizing for any reason.

Eventually whites regained complete control of the South and African-Americans were considered second-class citizens.

The Republicans who had once wooed the African-American vote no longer supported them. Pres. Rutherford B. Hayes toured the South and tried to encourage white people to respect blacks and let them vote. After it was obvious he was being ignored, he finally declared that the protection of the African-Americans' rights was in the hands of intelligent white men. Even the president could not change the minds of racist whites who were determined to return blacks to a powerless condition in America.

Chapter 8
Politics and Voting Rights

ARTICLE XV, UNITED STATES CONSTITUTION ELECTIVE FRANCHISE

Section I. The right of citizens of the United States to vote shall not be denied or abridged by the United States, or by any State, on account of race, color, or previous condition of servitude.

Section 2. The Congress shall have power to enforce this article by appropriate legislation.

Blacks tried to obtain parity with whites by becoming involved in politics during Reconstruction. They learned that voting was a very important part of the so-called democratic process. Thanks to the Supreme Court, the highest court in the land, their efforts to vote were thwarted.

The Ku Klux Klan threatened blacks in the South when they attempted to vote, and the Supreme Court's decision stated that the federal government was not required to become involved. If further stated that it was the state, not the federal government, that was required to guarantee protection of its citizens. The court did not suggest any ways to make the state protect its citizens, however, so the Klan was free to continue to openly threaten and harm black people without punishment.

The Supreme Court decision virtually told blacks that many privileges that whites enjoyed were not meant to be enjoyed by blacks.

Congress passed a civil rights bill that supposedly protected blacks against segregation in railroads, restaurants, theaters, and other places of public amusement. The court did not enforce these laws, however, and shortly after its passage, the Supreme Court declared the Civil Rights Act of 1875 unconstitutional.

After this act of the Supreme Court, individual states began passing segregation laws. They started out by segregating theaters, restaurants, and the hotels. They went on to practice segregation on trains. Even though blacks paid the same fare that whites paid, they were forced to sit in the smoking and baggage cars. These segregation laws were called Jim Crow laws at that time, and soon the entire South was segregated again.

When blacks filed charges of discrimination with the Interstate Commerce Commission, the Commission decided that there should be equal accommodations for both the races.

In spite of this decision, accommodations remained separate and were by no means equal on the trains. When some blacks in New Orleans decided to test the Jim Crow law of segregation on the trains before the Supreme Court, they used a light-skinned black by the name of Homer Plessy. He was allowed to ride in the train cars designated for whites until they discovered he was actually a black man. When he took his case to the highest court in the land (the Supreme Court), he lost (Plessy versus Ferguson). The judge decided Plessy's civil rights had not been violated, and blacks continued to be segregated by whites all over the South from then on.

Blacks were not allowed to participate in the electing of local or federal officials; therefore, they could not expect anything from the elected officials. Most of the elected officials were segregationist and were expected to deal with black issues in favor of whites or their time in office would be short-lived.

Without the support of the court and the lawmen, blacks had nowhere to turn. They found themselves at the mercy of the racist men that had previously owned them and that felt blacks were second-class citizens.

Segregating blacks from whites was one of the first ways blacks were denied their equal rights under the law in America. Denying them the right to vote was a sure way to keep blacks out of the decision-making process of local and national government.

Various methods were used to make sure blacks did not vote. Blacks were threatened, beaten, and even killed if they insisted upon voting on election days. Sharecroppers were no longer allowed to remain on white farms if they chose to vote. Whites watched the polls closely, and blacks who attempted to vote were blackballed by white merchants and other whites in the community. This sometimes meant that if a black attempted to vote, he could no longer be sure he could buy food at the local grocery store or even have a place to stay. Polling places were often deliberately set up in white neighborhoods where blacks were not allowed. They would change the polling place at the last minute and not inform blacks of the new location. Blacks would have strange accidents in their attempts to locate the ballot boxes.

Some ballot boxes were stuffed with names of people that did not exist. When this took place or when votes were miscounted (always in the favor of the white candidate), blacks had no recourse as there were no black poll-watchers. Here again, blacks could not depend on the local law officers, because in most cases they too were elected by the white community and were expected to be on the side of the people who had elected them.

In states where blacks were in the majority, laws were passed to keep blacks from voting. A convention was held in

1890 to find ways to disfranchise blacks or keep blacks from voting. At this convention it was suggested that a two-dollar poll tax be paid in advance before a person could vote. Two dollars were hard to come by at that time, and most blacks could not afford to pay this amount to vote.

Also, persons who had been convicted of a crime such as arson, burglary, bigamy, theft, or perjury could not vote. After blacks were freed, with nothing and nowhere to go, many of them found themselves being arrested at one time or another for one or two of these crimes. Some of them who had no criminal record at all were given one in order to prevent them from voting.

In addition, persons who could not read parts of the Constitution and interpret what they had read to the satisfaction of the white man in charge of polling places were not allowed to vote. Many of the poll-watchers were illiterate, and in cases where blacks read designated parts of the Constitution accurately, the white poll-watchers would tell them their interpretation of it would not be accepted.

White people did not have to follow these rules, of course, and even if they pretended to, black people were not allowed to watch the polls. Well-educated blacks were turned away while illiterate whites were allowed to vote.

Other ways were employed to stop blacks from voting, such as requiring them to own property and requiring them to read whatever a white poll-watcher insisted that they read. They used systems such as gerrymandering, where large populations of black votes were diluted by combining their vote with a larger number of white votes.

They used methods such as the grandfather clause. If a person's grandfather had qualified to vote by 1867, the person was allowed to vote. This was highly unlikely for a black person who had just been freed a couple years before.

After facing so many obstacles in attempting to gain the right to vote, blacks felt defeated and felt they were destined to be governed by white elected officials who in many cases had been elected to keep the African-Americans in their place.

Politics in America through the years has proven to use the most effective methods devised by whites to keep blacks from achieving equal justice. When there have been cases where blacks have been allowed to use their right to vote and are elected to decision-making positions, the purse strings are still controlled by the white power structure, relegating black elected officials to being nothing more than "paper tigers."

Chapter 9
Sharecropping

After blacks were freed, their first desire was to own some land and make a life for themselves and their families. Some say they had been promised "forty acres and a mule." It was also debated whether blacks should be the skilled laborers in America and leave the professional world to the whites.

In many cases, blacks bought land that had been sold, abandoned, or claimed by the government for failure to pay taxes. But Pres. Andrew Johnson ordered blacks to give this land up. (Even the president of the United States did his share to keep blacks from helping themselves.) This put blacks right back in the position they were in when they were supposedly freed. Some of them were forced to remain on the same farm they were on during slavery in order to survive. Some had to return to farm work for food and bare necessities, while some others chose to flee to the city in search of jobs.

Most blacks had no money, so they could not own their own farms. This is how sharecropping came about. The white man who had the money allowed the black man and his family to live on his plantation and farm the land. The white owner furnished the land while the black was expected to furnish the labor, tools, fertilizer, work animals, et cetera. The black man would have to begin by borrowing money from the white man to set up operations. He began in the hole, and the white man made sure he remained in the hole from then on. When the crop was harvested, the black man had to pay the white man from the money earned. He seldom earned enough to maintain himself and his family throughout the winter. This was a new form of slavery.

Chapter 10
Migration from the South

Less than ten years after blacks were supposed to have been freed, they were facing destitution. They were hungry and jobless, and the few who had farms were having little success with their crops. Blacks were being forced to leave the South by the thousands in order to survive. Blacks migrating in such large numbers caused whites to become concerned that possibly a conspiracy was taking place. Black labor had been an investment in the South, and whites who had built an empire with this free labor were not going to stand idly by and watch their investment walk away. They did not intend for blacks to have any power or status, but they definitely were accustomed to their performing the menial jobs in the South. White men and women had felt that free black labor was a fact of life, and the white power structure thought it was their duty to stop blacks from migrating from the South. The fact that blacks had the nerve and the ability to organize and do something on their own was also disturbing to white men. They were leery of these ex-slaves who had been totally dependent on them a few years ago and were now working together to perform a task. Stopping blacks from organizing was these whites' primary job, but they also had to stop blacks from learning how to work together.

Two black men whom the whites felt were somewhat responsible for blacks migrating from the South were called before a congressional committee for questioning. They were Henry Adams and Benjamin "Pap" Singleton. Adams, who seemed to have been under duress, said, "In 1870, I believe ... a parcel of us got together . . . to organize ourselves into a committee and look into ... the true conditions of our race, to see whether it was possible we could stay under a people who had held us under bondage Some of the members of the committee was ordered . . . to go into every state in the South where we had been slaves ... and post one another about the true conditions of our race.... The information they brought to us was very bad. They said in several parts where they was that the land rent was still higher there and the people was still being whipped, some of them by the old owners, the men that had owned them as slaves, and some of them was being cheated out of their crops. Some of them stated that in some parts of the country were they voted they would be shot." Adams told the panel why blacks were encouraged to leave the South in the first place:" along in August sometime in 1874, after the white league sprung up, they organized and said this is a white man's government and the colored men should not hold any offices; they were no good but to work in the fields and take what they would give them and vote the Democratic ticket. That's what they would make public speeches and say to us, and we would hear them. We then organized an organization called the Colonization Council. The congressmen learned that the Colonization Council planned to appeal to the president of the United States and to Congress to help them out of their distress, or protect them in their rights and privileges. And if that failed, their plan was to ask for some land in the United States for blacks, somewhere they could go and live with their families. If Congress would not give them land, the organization planned to ask Congress for money to help get black people to Liberia, a free black country in Africa. If Congress refused, they planned to ask foreign governments for help.

Adams said the council felt, by 1877, that it was time for blacks to leave the South, because it appeared that the racist conditions they were facing were not changing. He further stated, "The time got so hot down there they stopped our churches from having meetings after nine o'clock at night. They stopped them from sitting up and singing over the dead, and so forth ... and after they all did this, and we say it was getting so warm—killing our people all over the country, there were several of them killed right down in our parish—we appealed.... We had much rather stayed there if we could have had our rights.... In 1877 we lost all hopes.... We found ourselves in such conditions that we looked around and we seed that there was no way on earth, it seemed, that we could better our condition there, and we discussed them thoroughly in our organization along in May. We said that the whole South—every state in the South—had got into the hands of the very men that held us slaves—from one thing to another and we thought that the men that held us slaves was holding the reins of government over our heads in every respect almost, even the constable up to the governor.... In regard to the whole matter that was discussed, it came up in every Council. Then we said there was no hope for us and we had better go."

Blacks began to leave the South in large groups, going to all parts of the country. They were seeking jobs, voting rights, and the opportunity to live in peace with their families.

Blacks settled in the states of Kansas and Oklahoma in great numbers. They were welcomed at first, but white people soon became upset with the blacks who were flooding their cities, so they pushed to stop others from entering.

In Boley, Oklahoma, blacks established their own community. This city continues to be almost entirely black until this day.

It has been said that the white man allowed African-Americans to live rather peacefully in the state of Oklahoma because it was mostly a territory of mud. They changed their minds and took the land when oil was discovered. Boley, Oklahoma, continues to be a rare exception in America.

Prohibition of Slavery in California

ARTICLE I. Section 18, California Constitution of 1849
Neither slavery nor involuntary servitude, unless for the punishment of crime, shall ever be tolerated in this state.

African-Americans migrated to the free state of California, where they needed a white man to vouch for them in order to enter and remain in the state. This was against the will of most white men in California, who thought California should be a sanctuary for white people. In spite of this, the Prohibition of Slavery in California (Article I) was accepted unanimously by the committee on the constitution when they drew up the Declaration of Rights for California.

California lawmakers also proposed at the same time a law prohibiting free blacks from migrating and settling in California. This section would make it illegal for slave owners to bring slaves into the state and set them free. They were afraid that slave owners who came to California to mine gold would "strike it rich" and let their slaves go free. The lawmakers' rationale was that white people of California would end up having to feed these people, who would probably become vagrants.

Most of the politicians agreed that blacks would be unsightly in California. They felt this beautiful land was given to white people by God and it should be kept clean and free from being contaminated with lazy, uneducated, thriftless Negroes.

The congressmen thought blacks would work for low wages and white men would be forced to do likewise. If they kept blacks out, they would keep the wages on a high level for whites only.

African-Americans were brought up to the free state of California over all of the objections of the white men there. Most of them were brought in by white men who were too lazy to mine the gold themselves. Many of them were left there, as had been expected, after their owners "struck it rich." African-Americans who were left in California were treated harshly and often run out of the state by unsympathetic whites—policemen, judges, and hostile white men in general. Many of them ran to what they considered to be safer places within the state.

Los Angeles (the City of Angels) was one of the places African-Americans settled, and they felt they were safe from white men there. They remained there for only a short while before whites decided to invade the area and take it over.

Blacks were having such a hard time even in the so-called free state of California that they were forced to petition the U.S. Congress and ask them to help blacks colonize in some other country where their color would not be "a badge of degradation." These blacks were of the opinion that separation of the races would be good for the blacks and the white race.

Many blacks migrated on their own to Canada; Mexico; Baja, California; and Central America after no action was taken on their petition.

Most blacks refused to leave California, however, and others continued to come to the state, looking for the promised land. They dreamed of finding gold and living with their own people, free from segregation and discrimination.

A black man named Allensworth founded the California Colony and Home Promotion Association to lay the groundwork for the creation of a black town for the black people in the San Joaquin Valley. When he learned that the water supply was adequate and the land in the valley was reasonably priced, he began making plans for creating a black township. The community of Allensworth became a reality on August 3, 1908. An editorial in the county paper stated that Allensworth Township was created "in order to enable black people to live on an equity with whites and to encourage industry and thrift in the race."

In spite of the fact that the town was successful and blacks were doing for themselves, whites would not allow Allensworth to continue to exist. White men supposedly put strychnine in the water system and poisoned the water used by the entire township.

Allensworth Township was turned into a state national park and continues to be to this day.

The flow of black people from the South continued for many years. As expected, white southerners did not like the exodus of blacks from the South. Where would they get their cheap labor supply without a large black population? They tried to keep black people from leaving. Black leaders of the western movement were threatened and sometimes hurt. Penalties were heavy for blacks who broke old vagrancy laws or who disregarded labor contracts. Whites who encouraged black people to leave also were punished. Some counties hired out blacks to make sure that debts or penalties for crimes were paid. Sometimes these debts were passed from generation to generation, making it impossible for those hired out to leave. Other whites tried to encourage blacks to remain in the South by promising them high wages and better treatment, but blacks continued to leave the South by the thousands.

Unfortunately for most blacks, life was no easier in their new homes. Most of them continued to be extremely poor and in great need of help.

Blacks lost track of family and friends in migrating from place to place; they also lost the oneness they had felt with one another. Being separated as they were from friends and loved ones often made them suspicious of each other and selfish. There was not as much unity among blacks who were striving to get ahead at any cost. Blacks became divided and became more vulnerable to their enemies. Even though whites fought blacks migrating from the South, they ended up being the winner in that "a house divided cannot stand."

Chapter 11
World War I

When World War I began, white people immediately became concerned about blacks being armed. Here they had to trust men that they had been treating like animals with guns in their hands. They knew that, once armed, the black men might consider the white men to be his greatest enemies and turn the guns on them.

Some blacks felt they should not fight a war for America for a different reason. They had not been allowed to live in this country in peace with equal housing, adequate jobs, or equal opportunities. They felt it was inconsistent to expect a man who had been treated in such a harsh manner to be patriotic and want to defend this country.

Of course, there were other blacks who urged the white establishment to use black troops in this First World War. Most whites felt this was a time for red-blooded white Americans to display their patriotism and bravery. There were still other whites who thought it was a pity to waste white soldiers on the front lines when there were blacks begging to die for America. They were well aware of how blacks had fought and died in other wars America had been engaged in, but this was a world war, in which America would be playing an important role.

Blacks all over the United States began petitioning the government to draft blacks to fight. They formed their own marching groups, gave them fancy names, and competed against each other in the streets on Sundays. They begged to be recognized at least by the National Guards. No southern states had black National Guard units.

Though blacks flocked to recruiting stations when the war first broke out, they were turned down, especially in the South. This meant that blacks had to fight in America for the right to fight in World War I.

Military leaders did not know what to do with the black troops that were already in the army. They had a surplus of black soldiers in the Ninth and Tenth Calvary Regiments and the Twenty-fourth and Twenty-fifth Infantry Regiments, the only four black units in the army.

Nevertheless, when the Selective Service Act, which ordered the registration of every able-bodied male from twenty-one to thirty-one years of age, was passed, whites found themselves facing the problem of what to do with blacks who registered. The jobs in supply, manual labor, gravedigging, baking, truck driving, et cetera, that were reserved for blacks were all overstaffed.

Percentagewise, more blacks were finally drafted in the war than whites. There were few blacks in the army air corps, however, and blacks were barred from the marines completely. The marine corps was supposedly a select group of rough, tough, courageous, all-American men. Black were already all of these things and would have taken the fun out of it for the white boys.

Black jobs in the navy were limited to cooking, deck scrubbing, kitchen duty, et cetera. The navy was considered to be America's finest, patterned after England's Royal Navy.

Racial discrimination toward black soldiers was as bad in the army as it was at home, if not worse. Because of the attitudes of the whites in communities near black army camps, blacks were often restricted to the company area. They were even refused the use of most base facilities and were referred to derogatorily as "coons," "niggers," and "darkies" by white officers. They were forced to work under the most devastating and abusive conditions.

Treatment of the black soldiers was inhuman in that they were made to live in tents without floors or heat. They build the wooden barracks the white soldiers lived in. One winter, blacks at Camp Alexander in Virginia froze to death in their tents because they had only been issued lightweight fatigues. Seldom did they have adequate medical, recreational, or social facilities. National service organizations such as the Red Cross, Salvation Army, and YMCA virtually ignored the black soldier.

Black officers were required to wear enlisted men's uniforms during the week. They could wear their officer's uniform on Sundays and when they were on leave. Most of the time they had to salute white officers even if they outranked them.

Because of racism, inevitably blacks clashed with whites both in the military and in the communities. Most of the problems stemmed from the whites' objections to blacks wearing a uniform and representing America for a cause. The uniform itself seemed to have given blacks credibility. Blacks appearing as human beings in America represented a threat to most whites who felt blacks were hardly more than dumb animals.

The riot in Houston, Texas, was one of many riots that took place between black servicemen and whites. Black troops were stationed just outside the city of Houston for training. They had experienced weeks and weeks of racial slurs and discrimination. Black troops could take no more and were ready to strike back. They did not believe they should have to ride on segregated streetcars and endure brutal treatment from the people and the police. Their weapons had been confiscated earlier for fear that they might retaliate against Houston's whites.

When a black military policeman asked a white Houston policeman to explain why he was arresting a black woman for only using abusive language, the policeman said he didn't answer to Negroes. The white man struck the military policeman over the head and shot at him as he fled. Seventeen whites were killed before the riot ended. Thirteen blacks were sentenced to hang for murder and mutiny, and forty-one others were given life imprisonment.

Whites also talked against the black troops who were fighting with the French soldiers overseas. French officials were warned, through documents such as the one labeled "Secret Information Concerning Black American Troops," that black soldiers were innately inferior, that they were prone to vice, especially rape, that the French must not "spoil" them with too much evidence of democracy, and that French officials should stifle any expression of intimacy between the black troops and white French women.

Despite gross and overt acts of segregation and discrimination and repeated attempts by the Germans to persuade black troops to desert, America's black fighting men established an enviable record for bravery and heroism during World War I.

World War I ended on November 11, 1918, at eleven o'clock in the morning.

Black soldiers who went overseas could only receive the French Croix de Guerre because they only fought in combat with French soldiers. American white soldiers refused to fight with black American soldiers, and U.S. awards for bravery were reserved for white soldiers that had served their country no more gallantly than the black soldiers. Blacks received no American medals for bravery during World War I.

It is also alleged that officials from the United States met with the black soldiers while they were still in France, not to commend them, but to tell them that they would be returning to America and would not be expected to bring any of the French women back with them. They also supposedly told them not to come back to the States flourishing their uniforms and French medals in front of the white population. Black soldiers were given two weeks after their discharge to be out of the army uniform and into civilian clothes.

Immediately upon returning to the United States, black soldiers returned to second-class citizenship. Fighting in World War I had proved to be no more beneficiary to them than fighting in any of the other wars for America.

Chapter 12
Consistent Racism and Violence

> *"I am just as much opposed to Booker Washington as I am to voting by the cocoanut-headed, chocolate colored typical little coon, Andy Dotson, who blacks my shoes every morning. Neither one is fit to perform the supreme functions of citizenship."*
>
> —Sen. James Vardaman of Mississippi

Such a derogatory statement as the one cited above from such a high office could only be made about a phenomenon such as blacks were considered to be in America.

Lynching black people, though cruel and inhuman, was not a crime in America. White people who thought otherwise were obliged to keep quiet, because the popular opinion was "the only good nigger is a dead nigger."

There were 3,437 blacks brutally lynched between 1882 and 1951. The very idea that innocent people were being killed because of their color a hundred years after they were supposed to have been freed is utterly preposterous.

Black people were brought to this country and made into the monster that the white man desired them to be. Whites' resentment of blacks even being considered people was very apparent before they were freed. Shortly after the Civil War, forty-six blacks were killed in Memphis, Tennessee, because whites resented blacks returning to the South wearing uniforms and looking like real human beings. During this riot, the black section of town was burned down and innocent blacks were forced to flee for their lives.

In Wilmington, North Carolina, whites misinterpreted a black newspaperman when they thought he had written an article that showed lack of respect for white womanhood. On November 10, 1898, more than four hundred whites invaded the black section of Wilmington. Blacks were forced to flee from their homes, which were burned down, and more than thirty blacks were killed. Evidence was found later to indicate the riot had been well planned in advance.

In 1906, blacks in Atlanta, Georgia, had to seek refuge at the black colleges in attempt to save their lives. Hundreds of blacks were beaten when whites decided blacks who were supposedly getting out of hand needed to be taught a lesson. This riot lasted for more than three days, and the entire city had to be shut down.

Black soldiers were again victims in August 1906 during the Brownville, Texas, riot. Two white men had been shot previously. and though the black soldiers of the Twenty-fifth Infantry had not been in the area at the time of the murders, they were charged with the killings. The assailants were later positively identified, but not in time to stop the white uprising. White policemen declared open war on innocent soldiers, and the white community of Brownville assisted them. Worst of all, the president of the United States, Theodore Roosevelt, dishonorably discharged the entire Twenty-fifth Infantry Division. (This indicates again that the various presidents of the United States were in the forefront in aiding the racial violence that blacks had to endure.)

Pres. Woodrow Wilson let the nation know where he stood with the race issue by segregating all of the federal facilities in Washington, D.C. Throughout the history of blacks in America, it is interesting to note that racism has been upheld or ignored completely by the highest to the lowest officials in the various administrations. Blacks have had to withstand and attempt to get around this institutionalized racism. Resisting racism in America usually proves to be detrimental to one's health.

In Springfield, Illinois (the hometown of Pres. Abraham Lincoln), racial tensions were high in 1908 because of the influx of blacks that had migrated there from the South. Blacks were being used as strike breakers, and whites were losing their jobs. When tension became so high, white mobs destroyed the black section of town. Whites claimed a black handyman had raped a white woman, though it was later discovered this was just a false rumor. Eight black people were killed, and more than two thousand blacks fled the city in order to save their lives. The white population of Springfield later staged an economic and political boycott to drive the remaining blacks out of the city. They also threatened the lives of whites who refused to fire blacks who tried to remain in Springfield.

It might be interesting to note that it was after this particular riot that a white woman by the name of Mary White Ovington decided somebody should do something about white violence perpetrated on blacks and initiated the organizing of a group that later became known as the National Association for the Advancement of Colored People (NAACP).

Murdering black people during riots in America for a long time was not a crime, especially since most of the murderers were white. Seldom if ever was anyone punished for murdering a black, no matter how brutal the murder was. Whites could always get the law and most of the people in the community to agree that killing a black was "justifiable." For these reasons, blacks lived in constant fear of being killed. In most of the cities in America, a black was "damned if he did and damned if he didn't." Ironically enough, blacks did not display hostility or seem to be angry with their oppressors, though there were many similar incidents of oppression. They had no real disdain for America and continued to feel that one day things would be different for them. They had been so thoroughly indoctrinated during slavery to be loyal and religious. Blacks were so accustomed to enduring pain and hardship that they felt life was supposed to be that way. Most blacks never knew when times weren't hard, so just being free gave them the courage to continue to struggle in spite of the odds.

Chapter 13
How I Learned about Racism

On July 22, 1931, I was born. This was just sixty-six years after the ratification of the Thirteenth Amendment. The remnants of slavery were still very present in my small black neighborhood in Clinton, North Carolina. Along with many of my friends, I had ringworm and had no idea where it came from. Some of the women and girls who had ringworm wore their hair cut short like men in order to better tend to their scalps.

I was taught by my parents to say, "Yes, sir" and "No, sir" to grown-ups, and I noticed they would often say it themselves, especially to white people. We were also taught to go to the back door when we were sent to a white person's house for whatever reason. We were told to take off our hats when talking to white people, especially white women. Black men who were tall would often stoop when talking to a white man in order not to appear to be towering over him. White men did not like looking up to a Negro.

In 1931 the depression was in full swing. I didn't know it then, but blacks were not affected very much by the depression. They had no big-paying jobs, no big houses and bank accounts to lose. The stock market meant very little if anything to them.

They had small plots of land that most of them had inherited from their parents. They had houses that many of them had built themselves with the help of neighbors and friends. Black people survived with cows, hogs, a garden, and flour for bread.

My father worked at Mr. Henry Vann's auto garage during the depression. According to Daddy, his weekly salary had once increased to twelve dollars, but was brought down to four dollars during the depression. He said he overheard Mr. Vann tell another man that he was fortunate to have gotten his money and his family's money out of the bank in time before the banks went broke. Though Mr. Vann had not lost his money, he still cut my father's salary, which was already the lowest salary on the payroll. The reason my father left the garage, however, was because the foreman told him he wanted to come to his house every morning around 5:30 A.M. to make a fire in his fireplace. He told Daddy he could make the fire himself, but he just wanted to see how it felt to get up by a fire that a "nigger" made.

During the depression, many whites were as hungry and destitute as blacks. The only difference was when the depression was over, they were still white and were able to get good-paying jobs again.

Chapter 14
My Introduction to Fear and Violence

I remember hearing that Bill Simms had raped a white girl and he had to be moved to Raleigh to keep the Ku Klux Klan from lynching him. I had no idea what or who the Ku Klux Klan was or why the man was being moved to the capital. It seem Mr. Simms had been giving the white girl liquor from his father's stash and she was giving him sex in return. Mr. Brewington Williams, a black man, came upon them while they were having sex, and just as in the time of slavery, he went downtown and told the sheriff. Of course the girl claimed she had been raped, and Mr. Simms went to jail. All I remember was the fear that engulfed our neighborhood. Bill Simms was sentenced to life in prison.

Slave Labor

I remember when my mother and all of the other women in the neighborhood worked on Mr. Henry Moore's farm. I never knew why he hired very few men. When he didn't need the women, he would hire them out to his son Saul.

Henry Moore would come to our street around five o'clock in the morning and load his trailer with black women and children. He would return them when it was dark. In the summertime, darkness didn't come until after nine o'clock in the evening. Mother would return home tired and worn out from chopping and toiling long hours in the fields. Many days she worked for thirty five cents a day.

The only time we were allowed to go with Mother was during cotton picking time. Mr. Henry paid thirty-five cents per hundred pounds. Most of the women picked a little more than one hundred pounds, meaning that most of them earned a little better than thirty-five cents per day. I remember the cold mornings riding on the trailer. If your cap blew off, you would have to pick cotton in the hot open field all day without a cap. Mother warned us continuously to hold onto our caps. The sun would actually cook your scalp if you didn't wear a cap or some other form of protection on your head. There were few if any trees in the cotton fields, because cotton needs plenty of sunshine. I remember when people would fall down from too much sun. They would really be having sunstrokes, but no one in the fields knew it. They would douse them with the drinking water that was buried in the sand in a mason jar at the end of one of the cotton rows. (The water had been buried to keep it as cool as possible.) When the person would regain a little strength, he would return to the field, hot sun and all. All of this would take place in about fifteen or twenty minutes, and the person would resume working with little or no apparent ill effects from the sunstroke.

I recall very vividly how the older women would decide when it was quitting time and would send one of the younger children to the house to tell Mr. Henry we were ready to weigh up for the day. He would seem to purposefully wait until it was almost dark to come and see how much cotton everyone had picked. I had picked exceptionally hard one day in an attempt to pick at least one hundred pounds for once. I had only picked sixty-five pounds, according to Mr. Henry, and I thus had made less than thirty-five cents for the day's work.

Mr. Henry would pay the hands each evening with "tin chips" and redeem them on Saturday evening when he was ready. If a hand didn't work all week and on Saturday if Mr.

Henry wanted him to, he would not come by your house on Saturday to redeem your tin chips. If there was a half-cent involved, he took the half. Worst of all, he would not come around Saturday evening until late. Many of the stores downtown had closed by the time he came around, and I think he knew this. I remember sitting on the front porch watching for Mr. Henry many a Saturday evening for Mother.

I'll never forget when Miss Rachel, an old worker who had worked her fingers to the bone for Mr. Henry and his son Saul, was told to get off the trailer. She had gotten on the trailer that morning as usual, but Mr. Saul had told her to get off, because she was too old to work anymore. She refused to get off, thinking that old man Henry would stand up for her. When we got to the fields, Mr. Henry came out to the trailer and told Miss Rachel she was too old and had no business getting on the trailer since Mr. Saul had told her not to. She cried as she began the five-mile walk back home. All the other hands thought it was a shame, but dared not speak up for fear they would have to join her.

I remember being happy when the tractor overturned and killed Mr. Saul. He was very mean to his farmhands and seldom, if ever, smiled.

Chapter 15
My Introduction to Segregation

I can remember as though it was yesterday when they got a city bus line for the town of Clinton. They gave Clinton residents free rides continuously all over the city for two days. Blacks were informed that their seats were the last four seats in the back of the bus. This was very confusing to me at the time, because the evening before only blacks had been on the bus. We filled the last four seats in the bus and had to stand in the aisles, though all the other seats were empty.

One Black Hero

I still remember our first radio. It ran on batteries and in order to save the batteries, we could only turn it on to listen to certain programs. We would especially save the batteries for the Joe Louis fights, though it seems they would always be coming from Michigan and there would be so much static that we could never get the station clearly. We would have to go down to Mr. Arthur Frye's house to hear the fight, because he had a big radio. Joe Louis was the heavyweight champion of the world, a hero to all blacks. He was the only black in the world who had legal permission to hit a white man. I can recall the boxing match between Joe Louis and Max Schmeling when America was at war with Germany. White Americans cheered for Max Schmeling, the German, instead of Joe Louis, the American. Blacks would foolishly laugh at Joe Louis, because he was said to be dumb. It was also common knowledge that white folks took his money and left him answering to Internal Revenue. He had to continue to fight even after he was washed up, because he was broke. I thought later that this was how white America taught lessons to blacks who thought they could beat them and get away with it.

It still saddens me to think of the first time I saw Joe Louis on television. It was in Augusta, Georgia, in 1951, and he was fighting Rocky Marciano. Marciano knocked Joe Louis completely out of the ring. This was a sad day for all black Americans. Our one black hero was gone.

Chapter 16
More Segregation

We black elementary-school students had to walk past the big white elementary-school to get to our little school for blacks. The black school had grades one through twelve all in one building. I recall one of our jobs during the first days of school was to erase the names of the white students from the books that were handed down to us from the white schools. We also had to repair many of the books that had backs and pages missing. Though we were led to believe that only black students were destructive, the microscope in my science class during my senior year in high school was a broken one that had been passed down to us from the white high school.

The state gave the white high school new equipment, new books, and new material each year. White school board officials issued to the black school used books, equipment, and materials from the white school. This system was called "separate but equal," and blacks were expected to compete on the same level with whites while using inferior equipment, et cetera. I was not aware at the time of all of the things the white students were getting that we weren't. It was only apparent when it came time to compete with them.

Chapter 17
Segregation within the Black Race

I was very sad when I wanted to play the lead role in a play in elementary school and did not get the part supposedly because I was too black. This was racism from within my own race, so naturally I didn't recognize what was happening. I wanted to be the Naughty Rabbit who was the star of the play. I knew I was the smartest boy in the class and definitely thought I deserved the part. After K. W. Butler got the part, I was told by Mrs. Janet Maynor that K. W. was more suitable because he had lighter skin. According to her, the role of the little Brown Bear suited me better. Perhaps she was right, but in retrospect, I feel that was a bad way for a boy my age to learn about color.

Chapter 18
The White Woman as a Cause of Racism in America

I was little more than twelve years old when I joined the Boy Scout. One day Miss Tillie Hobbs fell right in front of my father's lumberyard, and being a Boy Scout, I was anxious to do a good deed for the day. Rescuing her would be a good deed; in fact, it would have been my best bet. It would be like saving someone's life. I was confused when Daddy grabbed me and said, "Don't touch her; let her lie there." I thought, *What on earth is he talking about. Here is a lady in distress, and he's saying let her lie there.* Daddy explained to me that Ms. Tillie was a white woman and I could get in trouble by putting my hands on her. He explained that black men had died just for touching white women. He said, "Let someone of her own color come and help her." I was very confused and baffled, because I didn't know what racism in America was all about. I had not been taught that there were black Boy Scouts and white Boy Scouts and black people and white people. I didn't know that black scouts did good deeds for black people and white scouts did good deeds for white people. I thought scouts were scouts and people were people. My father had not taught me about racism before.

I soon learned about racism in the Boy Scouts of America, when I went to the black scout camp the following summer. We went to Camp Carver in Goldsboro, North Carolina. I can't say I expected the camp to be integrated, because I was used to not mixing with members of other races. It would have been astonishing if the camp had been integrated, even though it was sponsored by the Boy Scouts of America. After all, nothing else was integrated. As a matter of fact, integration was against the law in America at that time.

We were apparently the first scouts to go to Camp Carver, because the camp was new and undeveloped. This was fine with us, and we did very well the first few days cleaning the dead branches from the lake, raking leaves, cutting down trees, and beautifying the area in general. One day we were blazing a trail when a terrible thunderstorm came up. We were deep in the woods and didn't know our way back to the camp. To our surprise, we ended up in the plush white Boy Scout camp on the other side of the lake. Camp Tuscarora was also in Goldsboro, North Carolina, but for white boys. It had a dining hall made from logs, and they had dishes, forks, and spoons. We had a tent at Camp Carver for a dining hall and ate from mess kits. The all-white campsite had a lake area that was already cleared out and a pool with clean, clear water in it. They had a beautiful surrounding area, and the scouts were lounging around as though they were at a summer resort. They looked like the scouts in my scout handbook—white, middle-class, and happy. They did not offer to help us find our way back to camp, though a scout is supposed to be helpful. They were even hostile toward us and acted as though we were foreigners intruding on their privacy.

When we found our way back to Camp Carver, it was not the same anymore. Our camp resembled the "unexplored jungle" compared to Tuscarora. I had seen another example of separate but equal according to white America. I was no longer really interested in the Boy Scouts anymore, because I didn't feel blacks could afford to be scouts. It appeared that the Boy Scouts was a middle-class white organization designed to teach white boys how to rough it. Black boys had little need to learn how to rough it. Many of them were already living like they were outdoors and had been roughing it all of their lives.

Chapter 19
Exploitation

I still grimace when I think of how white insurance men used to take advantage of people in our neighborhood when I was a child. Sometimes the insurance man would be in our neighborhood and my mother would hide when she didn't have any money to pay him. She would tell us to close the front door, and when he'd knock on the door, we would open it and tell him she was not at home. The insurance man would defy us and make us go and get Mother anyway. She would come to the door and tell him apologetically that she did not have any money. He would reprimand her for not having come to the door in the first place. He would feel free to sit on the porch or in the living room and stay as long as he wished. Back then, no black man could sit in a white woman's living room with her no matter how many children were present. The insurance man would use profanity or obscene words if he chose to, and we were obligated to grin. I learned later that mother had no idea what those insurance policies covered, though she had all of us insured. She had been paying a little something on them every week for as long as I could remember.

The insurance man would invariably order one of us to go and get him a glass of cold water or lemonade. When he was ready, he would tell Mother when he would be back and advise her to be home with the money. I would be relieved of the uneasy feeling that I had begun to get every time a white man was in my presence when he left. I was learning that white men were to be respected at all times, and I did not like it.

That same insurance man had everybody on Railroad Street insured. I learned later that blacks were very reverent when it came to funerals and burials. They had gotten this from their forefathers in Africa, who had definitely respected the dead. When Africans were brought to this country, they could not show the same respect and reverence for the dead, because they were made to leave Africa in Africa. On the boat to America, when an African died he was thrown overboard without ceremony. When a slave died, most of the time a hole was dug and the body was thrown in. The gravediggers would throw dirt directly in the dead person's face as one would with an animal. This was a traumatic experience for a people who thought of death as the final leg of their journey through life. They were used to making elaborate preparations for this journey. They spent a great deal of their lives getting ready for the time after death. (The great pyramids of Egypt are good examples of the preparation Africans made for death.)

After slavery was abolished, blacks, whenever possible, would have a ceremony for their dead. They would wash the dead body on what they called a cooling board and sit around the room. They would be paying their last respects to the dead. They would sit up all night with the body to fan the flies and keep the rats away. In the Deep South, the body would decay quickly, because most of the time it was hot and blacks had no way of embalming their dead.

Blacks looked forward to the day when they could afford what they called a decent burial. They thought that after a man or woman had lived such a hard life, a decent burial in a cool resting place was not much to ask for. It was thought to mean peace at last. Ceremonies after death was one thing blacks brought from Africa that they never forgot.

When white insurance men learned of blacks' attitude toward death, they came from everywhere with promises of a decent burial. I didn't know it then, but this was what we were experiencing when white insurance men came to our house.

Chapter 20
World War II

I remember my father was an air raid warden when World War II began. He was responsible for our street when the town of Clinton held air raid practices. I still recall when he would go outside at night to see to it that the neighbors' lights were out when the test alarm went off. (I don't know how the enemy could have seen our lights since we could hardly see by them inside the house. The only lights we had down by the railroad were kerosene lamps. We were proud of Daddy anyway, because he was doing something for his country.

When Daddy had to go to Fort Bragg to be examined for the army, we were somewhat disappointed when he failed the physical exam. The greatest thing that could happen to a black man was to go into the service. Old folks would say, "This will make a man outa him." It meant a steady salary and three square meals a day. It was a ticket out of the South and perhaps a trip overseas. I remember seeing the little flags in the window with stars to represent the number of sons a family had in the service at one time. This meant an allotment would be sent home to the family.

Goose pimples would come over me when a soldier was introduced in church during the Sunday morning service. I could hardly wait until I was old enough to join the army, because the girls seemed to be crazy about a man in uniform. The preacher would preach about the war and pray that America won and the boys would return home safely.

I hated Hitler, Mussolini, and Hirohito with a passion, because we were taught that these were America's enemies. I used to draw their pictures and enjoy destroying them. The school plays and songs were all patriotic, and we would cry at the movies when the white soldiers were killed. This was the least I could do for my country. The only way I ever saw a black soldier depicted as a hero was when he died to save a lot of white soldiers. Otherwise, I seldom if ever saw a black in a war picture.

I had no idea that the armed services were segregated. It never occurred to me that there was racism when two men were fighting for the same cause and country. I did not know that there was an army for black men and an army for white men in America.

I had heard black men talk about German prisoners being treated better than black soldiers when they both were down south. In fact, these men said black troops would have to pull the shades down on the troop train when riding through the South to keep from being jeered at by whites.

Yet the worst thing that could happen to a black man was to be classified 4F. This meant he had been turned down by the army and apparently was not in good physical condition. A 4F man would be whispered about in a crowd and was treated as though he had the bubonic plague by the folks in the neighborhood.

The following extract indicates just a few of the problems black servicemen and women faced:

> During the early months of the war blacks found it difficult to get jobs because unemployed whites were invariably hired first. The explanation usually given was that skilled workers were in demand and the majority of blacks were unskilled laborers. The first defense industry jobs opened to blacks were menial ones newly vacated by white workers who advanced to better paying positions in aircraft plants, shipyards, and other war related industries.

The federal government's attempts to discourage employment discrimination were confined largely to periodic statements urging employers to implement fair employment policies.

Under the Selective Service Act of 1940, more than three million black men registered for service in the armed forces. Largely because of educational deficiencies and discriminatory draft boards, however, the rate of rejection of blacks from the military was significantly higher than for whites. Reaching enlistment peak in September 1944, the various branches of the U.S. military counted 701,678 blacks in the Anny, 165,000 in the Navy, 5,000 in the Coast Guard, and 17,000 in the Marine Corps. Scattered in virtually all branches of the armed services were more than 4,000 black women. Of the blacks who were in uniform in World War II, approximately 6,000 were officers, including I brigadier general, 10 colonels, and 24 lieutenant colonels. In the Navy most black servicemen were assigned to mess duty; not until April 1942 did the Navy accept blacks for general service and as noncommissioned officers.

Serving in segregated units headed by white officers, black Army men worked in truck companies, port battalions, and work outfits, cleaning up debris, rebuilding cities, building fortifications, erecting camps, and performing similar tasks. Yet black soldiers also fought, as witness the twenty-one black combat units that saw action in European ground operations. Other black Army units served in the Mediterranean and Pacific theaters.

In January 1945, the U.S. Army announced the black and white troops would be integrated as a single fighting unit in Germany on a volunteer basis. The experimental unit was short-lived, however, as the war in Europe ended soon afterward, on May 17, 1945.

Blacks in the Army Air Corps were segregated in all black units when the War Department in June 1940 declared that blacks would be trained as pilots at Tuskegee, Alabama while black ground crews would receive their training at Chanute Field in Illinois. The result was that approximately six hundred black fighter pilots received their wings before the end of the war and saw action in Europe under the command of Colonel Benjamin O. Davis, Jr., winning the admiration of blacks everywhere.

Such liberalism was the exception to the rule, however; black servicemen were victims of discrimination everywhere, at home as well as abroad. Wartime conditions in the South were especially bitter for blacks who saw German prisoners of war allowed in restaurants and other places of public accommodation, while U.S. service men and women who were black were invariably turned away and even beaten by angry whites. Segregation was also the policy on military posts, with separate accommodations for whites and blacks strictly maintained. Discrimination on some bases even included a ban on black-published newspapers and black social activities. The official ending in July 1944 of racial segregation in all Army recreational and transportation facilities produced no change in the conditions black troops were subjected to in other areas of military life.

Attempts by black servicemen to resist the practices of discrimination and segregation resulted in innumerable clashes both on and off military bases. At Port Chicago in California, black servicemen, refusing to perform dangerous work assignments on grounds that they were being racially exploited, were arrested and charged with mutiny. Although blacks vigorously protested such treatment, sometimes in fatal encounters with white troops, their pursuit of justice was futile.

Despite many instances of individual heroism, no black servicemen who fought in either world war was awarded the Congressional Medal of Honor. An outstanding example of service worthy of the highest military honor was the action of Dorie Miller, a black seaman assigned to mess duty on the battleship Arizona at Pearl Harbor. Though untrained as a gunner, Miller shot down four Japanese planes on December 7, 1941. In earlier wars a number of black servicemen won the Congressional Medal, including sixteen black soldiers and five black sailors in the Civil War and seven black servicemen in the Spanish-American War. In the two world wars it appeared that the nation's highest military honor was reserved through some unaccountable regression in decency in white servicemen. Many black servicemen did receive presidential citations ranging from the Good Conduct Medal to the Distinguished Service Cross. Eighty-eight of the six hundred fighter pilots who flew in Europe were awarded the Distinguished Flying Cross for outstanding achievement in thirty-five hundred missions.

I remember when we got the word that the war was over. I was outside sweeping out Daddy's car. We jumped for joy and prepared for the homecoming of the boys who had been so brave.

It didn't take long for the veterans to get back in the flow of the southern way of life. They were well aware that they were back in Clinton when on Armistice Day the black veterans were virtually ignored in the parade that took place every year. Of course the black vets were in the back of the parade and the fanfare was over after the white veterans passed.

Chapter 21
The Woodyard

All of my adolescent and teenage life I helped my daddy work in his woodyard. That is how he made a living for the family. We got our wood from the Fess Turlington's Sawmill, free of charge. The deal between Daddy and Mr. Turlington was that Turlington would give us the by-products (strips and slabs) from the logs if we would keep them from piling up and getting in the way of the men at the mill. This was a thankless, dirty job that Daddy had inherited from his father. Daddy was small in stature, and working with the heavy wood was very taxing to his frail body. Daddy was a hardworking, determined person, however, and managed to make a very decent living in the lumberyard.

Daddy was ignored completely by most blacks and especially the white establishment, because they were sure he was not making enough money for them to worry about. As long as black people acted like they didn't have anything and did not dress fancy and buy big cars and houses, white people would not bother them. Though whites have always said blacks should help themselves, many systematically placed stumbling blocks in the way of any black who seemed to be making progress. Daddy played their game and won.

There were only two white men working at the mill. One of them drove the carriage, and it was his job to decide the size of the lumber. He was considered to be the only skilled laborer on the job, though most of the blacks performed very skillful jobs. He never communicated with any of the black workers on the job. He ate alone and was the overall boss of the mill. I don't recall anyone saying he was the boss, now that I think about it. I probably took for granted he was boss, for all of those years, simply because he was white.

The other white man there was named Mr. Love. He acted the same way the carriage man acted, though he was considered to be white trash. I don't quite know how blacks determined this, but he received little respect from them. Yet he knew he was white and felt he was better than the blacks on the job. He too ate alone and seldom if ever communicated with anyone else, including the other white man. I used to watch the two of them and wonder why they chose to live lonely lives on the job.

It seemed to me that the only two people that benefited from having served in World War II were the two Turlington boys. They were the sons of the white man that owned the mill. I had heard from the black workers at the mill that the boys were officers in the service, and when I first saw one of them I had goose pimples. He looked like the soldiers in the magazines. I wanted to grow up and look just like him. The other brother showed up a few days later, looking mean and grim. Neither of them ever bothered communicating with any of the black workers at the mill. As I recall, they never communicated with Mr. Love either. Every now and then, they would talk to the white man on the carriage; otherwise, they would treat the workers as though they were zombies. Word spread quickly among the black workers that things would be changing, because the boys were taking over the mill for their father. The old, alcoholic, and lazy men on the job were shaking and trying to shape up.

The first thing the new bosses did when they settled down on the job was begin charging Daddy for the wood we were getting from the mill. I must admit that I envied these boys, even though I did not know them. I had no idea if they had more formal education than I. (As a matter of fact, I was a sophomore in college at the time.) I think I was impressed with the idea that they were young, white, and in charge. I wanted very much to be their friend, but having been in the South all of my life, I understood that they were white and were not really supposed to be friendly with me. They spent their time quietly driving the workers and expanding the business. "More for less" seemed to have been their goal.

The workers had no benefits and no job security. Most of the workers' jobs were out in the open, where, as in the cotton fields, the sun was extremely hot. When any one of the workers was overcome by a heatstroke, it would be a joke among the other workers. I watched men stretched out on the ground with knots jumping around all over their body. None of the men knew that those clots were because the person was having a sunstroke. The sick person would be lifted by a couple of men and placed under a tree. A bucket of water would be dashed on his body already wet with sweat. When the person regained consciousness, he would be given a few minutes to recuperate and then had to return to work. If he could not return to work, he would be laid off or fired. Back on the job for the remainder of the evening, the other men would joke "da monkey got 'em."

Chapter 22
Mother's Job

Mother began working for Dr. Johnson after Mrs. Sweeter could no longer work. Even though Mrs. Sweeter had diabetes and had one leg removed as a result of it, she was angry with Mother for taking the job when she had to leave. She said the Johnsons were her white folks and she would ride to their house in her wheelchair daily, because she was so conditioned.

Dr. Johnson had sent Mrs. Sweeter's son to college for her, and she was obligated to work for him as long as she was able or as long as they wanted her. Dr. Johnson asked Mother to let him send me to college, but Mother refused. The doctor wanted to enslave her for life, as he had Mrs. Sweeter.

Mother worked for the doctor seven days a week for the total sum of three dollars a week. We children would meet her down the street when she was on her way home from work, and she would give us scraps that she had taken from the Johnsons' kitchen table. I especially loved the pork chop bones when Dr. Johnson and his wife had left some meat on them. As if we were little puppies, Mother would feed us out of the greasy bag from the big house.

As I grew older, I became aware that Mother was working like a slave for Dr. Johnson and was afraid to miss a day's work. I would try to talk her into quitting completely, but she would shudder at the thought. Every time I came home from college, her dedication to her bondage was more and more apparent. She would want to take off at least on Sunday when

I was at home, but wouldn't dare because she had to cook the Johnsons' Sunday dinner.

When I joined the army, one of my goals was to stop Mother from working for Dr. Johnson. I had an allotment made out to her so she would no longer have to work for him. The allotment was for thirty-five dollars per month, which was twenty-three dollars more than she was making per month with Dr. Johnson.

When I returned home from the army two years later, Mother was still working for the Johnsons. She was working all day, because she had to cook two meals a day, clean up the house, and perform an added duty— take care of Mrs. Johnson, who was now an invalid. Mother had to lift her from her bed to her chair and to the toilet. She was still afraid to quit. When I insisted that she stop working for the Johnsons the terror in her face was very vivid.

Finally, one day when Mother decided not to go to work, Dr. Johnson and his wife rode slowly down our street toward our house that very afternoon. Mother jumped up from the porch and ran into the house. She said, "Brother, here come Dr. Johnson and Mrs. Johnson. Tell 'em I ain't home." I had been used to defying white men in the army, so I was not afraid of the Johnsons. As I recall, I did become nervous as they rode slowly past the house. I composed myself as they turned around in our yard and came back to the front of the house.

I can still see that big fat Dr. Johnson when he said , "Tell Beatrice to come out here."

I said, in as strong a voice as I could, "She is not working for you anymore."

He snapped back, "Nobody asked you. I said get Beatrice out here."

I felt like a little boy, though I was twenty-three years old and a veteran. I felt even smaller when Mother crept out of the front door and walked down the steps to the Johnsons' car. I have no idea what they told her. I only knew that the next morning she was up bright and early and went to work for the Johnsons again.

Chapter 23
Dislike of My Own Hair

I remember when Uncle Joe came from New York with our Aunt Almira. He wasn't really our uncle, but we children were told he was so he could sleep in the same room with my aunt. Anyway, Uncle Joe promised to show me and my brother how to get waves in our hair. I was convinced that I had the kinkiest hair in the world, because I had to get a haircut every two weeks, whether I thought I needed one or not. I noticed that curly-headed blacks did not get haircuts that often. I had seen that even dark-complexioned blacks with curly or wavy hair fared better than plain black nappy-headed fellows. Light-skinned blacks with kinky hair had fewer problems within the race and fewer problems with white folks than did plain black kinky-headed fellows. I was learning that racism existed within the black race as well as with the white race. It was my ultimate wish to have straight, wavy, or curly hair. Frankly, this had to be the wish of every kinkyhaired black American, because we were so ostracized by our own peers.

Uncle Joe was light-skinned, tall, and considered handsome. As I recall, he had large, rough, awkward-looking hands because he worked in a New York junkyard. He probably was not handsome at all, but was considered to be simply because he was light-skinned and had straight black hair.

My brother and I thought Uncle Joe's hair was something else again, and we would sit and stare at it, wishing our hair was as attractive. Uncle Joe told us he could make our hair look the same way, and I thought my prayers had been answered. We could hardly wait until Uncle Joe fixed our hair.

The first thing Uncle Joe did was wash my head vigorously; then he put this thick hair pomade called Nu Nile all over my head. After packing my head with this heavy white grease, he took a towel that he had heated over the hot wood stove and put it on my head to melt the grease. He then got some black soot from the fireplace chimney and rubbed it over my head to make it black. He said, "Now check that out." I couldn't wait to see what my hair looked like. This was going to be the new me for the rest of my life.

When I looked at myself in my mother's mirror, I could see my hair was black. In fact, my whole head was black, thanks to the soot Uncle Joe had put all over it. I remember calling my sister to look for waves on the back of my head. When she thought she saw one wave on the back of my head, I had her to keep her finger on it until I got a little mirror from Mother's pocketbook. When I tried to position myself to see the wave with the two mirrors, I could not see it. I always wondered if it was ever really there.

I went to bed with a stocking cap on, trying to keep my hair looking the same until it was time for school the next morning. The soot ruined my mother's pillowcase. There was also soot on my neck, in my ears, and down my back before the night was over. I washed up the next morning, thinking of how my girlfriend would admire me now that my hair was different.

When I got to school, I waited for her to arrive. When I saw her bus coming, I positioned myself right by the bus door so she could see me when she got off the bus. The first boy off the bus was Robert Royal. He took his fingers and raked through my hair after he jumped from the bus. The white grease and soot looked like lard and dirt mixed together and was very nasty-looking. When I tried to remedy the situation by rubbing my hair back, my hands got greasy and sooty. My shirt collar was black with soot by then, and it seemed I was sweating more than ever. All in all, I had a very miserable day and was convinced that I would be nappy-headed all my life.

Chapter 24
Polarization of the Races

I remember the Clinton Theater, where blacks had to sit upstairs and whites sat downstairs. The upstairs where we sat was then divided into two sides, and the other side was for Indians. When a good movie was playing at the theater and few Indians were attending, the management would open up the Indians' side to blacks. White people were not allowed to come upstairs with the blacks, and by no means were black people allowed to go downstairs with the whites. Blacks could only buy popcorn through a little window cut in the wall of the main lobby. Whites entered the theater through the main lobby and was able to buy any of the knickknacks on sale. Blacks would not be served until all whites were served, and sometimes the clerk would just let a black stand at the hole and not serve him or her at all.

At that time, the most popular movies were Tarzan, King Kong, and Shirley Temple movies. Blacks who never went to the movies, like my mother and father, went to see those movies when they came to the Clinton Theater. Blacks applauded when Tarzan beat up tribes of Africans. We cried when Tarzan's life seemed to be in jeopardy and when things did not go right for his wife, Jane. Blacks cried for the white woman that was captured by King Kong. Blacks wore Shirley Temple curls on Sunday and for all special occasions. We admired Shirley Temple's ability to learn the tap dance steps that were taught to herby Bill "Bojangles" Robinson. The way whites saw it, she was tap dancing, while Bojangles was "buck dancing," even though he was the teacher.

Black people were not aware that they were laughing at themselves when they laughed at Steppin Fetchit, Beulah, Uncle Ben, Aunt Jemima, and Buckwheat. Little did they realize the media was presenting an image of blacks in America that would never be erased from the minds of the American people, black or white. By presenting blacks as "coons," lackadaisical, happy, shuffling idiots, movies etched in the minds of whites and blacks the idea that black fit that mold.

The movie, Birth of a Nation was the most devastating example of the degradation of blacks by the media, as the following paragraphs indicate:

> In the depiction of the Reconstruction, emancipated blacks are shown as ignorant, lustful villains; black congressmen are heavy drinkers who recline in legislative seats exposing bare feet as they lustfully ogle the white women in the gallery. According to Griffith, "carpeting rule" brought an even worse tyranny to the South than white landowners exercised when they were in power. Griffith's thesis as set forth in the film is that after the war, the wealthy, paternalistic white folk became victims living in fear of the plundering, raping, subhuman ex-slaves; it was this situation, posits the film, that created the Ku Klux Klan, an organization of ex-Confederate soldiers bent on intimidating and terrorizing blacks from office, the polls, and the streets. In one of the closing sequences of the film the Ku Klux Klan arrives just in time to save a white family barricaded against a mob of murdering blacks.

> In a short time a campaign to prevent the film's showing was launched with letters of protest followed by editorials in many black newspapers. Despite their efforts and similar protests across the country, blacks were unable to curb public acceptance of the film, especially in the South. After it was shown at the White House, the first movie ever to be screened there, President Woodrow Wilson was said to have

commented, "It is like writing history with lighting, and my one regret is that it is all so terribly true

Blacks who sell themselves to the media and depict negative images of their people have no idea the disservice they do to their race. Nellie Conley (Madam Sul-Te-Wan) was one of the first blacks to do this when she accepted a role in the racist film Birth of a Nation. "Madam Sul-TeWan, who had heard that a great number of colored people were going to be hired, appealed to the general manager of the Fine Arts Film Company for a bit part in the The Birth of a Nation. Recognizing her outstanding talent after the first day of filming, director D. W. Griffith raised her salary from three dollars to five dollars a day, and had the scriptwriters develop a special scene for her. The scene, showing her as a wealthy black woman who employed black servants on her estate, was the director's attempt to illustrate that some blacks were able to achieve success after emancipation. In the final editing of the film, however, this particular scene was cut as it did not project the image of blacks as inferior beings."*

My image of beauty in a woman was Ava Gardner, Elizabeth Taylor, and Kim Novak. Like everyone else that went to the movies, I naturally saw these women as beautiful, because white America had decided that this was what beauty in women would be. I used to dream about such women after I saw them in a love story on the screen. I looked forward to the day when I would grow up and have a beautiful girl like one of these women. The only black woman shown in the movies that looked as beautiful was Lena Horne. She would be made to look as white as possible, keeping the notion of light and white in focus. Seldom if ever did we see a dark-complexioned man or woman in the movies portrayed as beautiful. Yet when a black man was seen with a white woman or sort after the semblance of his movie idol, white America objected.

The media has done very little to portray positive images of blacks in order to correct some of the wrong thoughts most Americans have of them. In fact, the media can take a lot of the credit for the way Americans view black Americans. The media has always given the public what they seemed to want to see, hear, and read and what made it the most money. The damage has been done to the black race seems to have been irrelevant to the media.

Chapter 25
Teenage Memories

It brings chills to my body when I think of how we blacks had to buy ice cream and then leave the drugstore. On Sunday afternoon after church it was fashionable for boys to walk their girlfriends downtown to Joe Reynolds's Drugstore for ice cream. This was the only store that opened on Sundays and sold ice cream products. As I recall, buying ice cream was fashionable because white boys and girls did it. The difference was, they could sit and eat their banana splits or sundaes in the booths. Blacks had to go to the back of the drugstore to place their order and were sold ice cream only. When we made our purchase, we could not sit and eat in the store; we had to leave the store immediately and eat the ice cream in the streets. I can still see the frowns the young white girl would have on her face when she came to the back of the store to serve us.

As a Young Man

My ego would be deflated even then when I had to stand in Leder Brothers Department Store and wait for one of the white men to come and wait on me. Even though they would seldom be busy, they would purposefully wait awhile before coming over to wait on a black. They would glance at me when I entered the store and continue talking as though I weren't there . Invariably they would find something to laugh about, and of course I would feel the joke was on me. They would sometimes make a black wait five or ten minutes for no apparent reason. One of the department stores' motto for blacks was, "What you try on is what you buy." If a black person tried on a hat, whether it fitted him or her or not, he would have to buy it. White people did not want to try things on after a black had put it on. The clerk would show a black one or two items before becoming disgusted and terminating the possible sale. No matter how much money a black spent in the store, he or she was always treated as a stranger and hurried out of the store.

Disrespect

My best friend broke my collarbone while we were wrestling during the recess hour. I was rushed to Dr. Airy's office from the school playground. I had never been to a white doctor before. I was sure Daddy would have taken me to Dr. Sammons, the town's only black doctor.

Dr. Airy claimed he did not have the proper brace to put on my shoulder to assure that my collarbone would heal properly. He took some gauge cloth tape and wrapped it around my shoulder several times after setting the bone back in place.

When my mother came home from work, she was very sympathetic. More than that, she was concerned about whether she would have to stay home from work with me the following day. She felt that Dr. Johnson and his wife needed her no matter what had happened to me. To be sure my shoulder would not be sore enough to keep her from going to work, she rubbed it down with linament before she went to bed. She put linament under the cloth tape, which caused my skin to blister and irritate. The next morning she had to take off from work and take me to the doctor because of the blisters.

I can still feel the pain that I felt that morning when Dr. Airy took the old tape off and cleaned the blistered skin off my shoulder with rubbing alcohol. He had no pity on me when he reset the broken collarbone. The pain after one night was more than intense. He was cursing while he worked with no regard for the fact that Mother was in the room. I'll never forget his saying, "I wish these niggers would let me be the goddam doctor." I had never heard a grown-up curse in front of a lady before, black or white. I had lots of contempt for this doctor and have never trusted another white doctor to have my total interest at heart.

Silas Green and the Winstead Minstrels

I remember Silas Green and the Winstead Minstrels. Black faced acts were very popular during the forties, and blacks and whites could hardly wait until they came to town. I used to hear grown men arguing about which of the minstrels had the best acts or the prettiest girls.

"Silas Green from New Orleans-Best olesho you've ever seen."

The posters would go up all over town weeks before the minstrels were scheduled, so folks could get their money together. On the day of the show, like the circus, they would have a preview at twelve o'clock noon downtown. Black men with sooty faces and big white lips and beautiful scantily dressed women marched with the band from their tent to downtown. Children would leave school to go downtown for the preminstrel show. The show people would also come outside the tent about two hours before the show started to perform a few skits for the public, who would be waiting in big crowds to see the free entertainment. I had never seen such beautiful women with big, light-colored thighs. During each exhibition, white men with the show would sell snake oil and tonic that they said was good for everything.

Inside the tent, blacks had to sit on the sides in the bleacher seats. White people and light-skinned blacks who could afford it would sit in the scats down in the center of the tent. Dr. Murdick was the only black I can recall who was light enough and, thanks to the black community, had enough money to sit in the center with the whites.

The dancers' costumes were lined with sequins, and the women were all light-skinned and gorgeous. All the jokes were on the dark-complexioned show people (men and women) who were always dressed shabbily. Sometimes they would have a white man in the show, and of course he always outsmarted the blacks.

During intermission the show people would sell the same snake oil and worthless tonics.

Like Amos and Andy, black people had no idea what this was doing to them as a race. Clowning and making jokes on themselves was a carryover from slavery. Very little has changed in the entertainment world over the years. Blacks who sought or seek the glamorous world of entertainment and media would in some cases sell their souls and the dignity of their people for financial gains and prestige. The media and the entertainment world have done very little to change the portrayed image of the black man in America.

During and after slavery, blacks were accustomed to entertaining whites on all occasions and in many ways. Blacks were known to have exceptional rhythm, and tap dancing. even in the sand, became the American blacks' specialty. It was called buck dancing by white people, and of course it was not considered to be a cultured dance, compared to the waltz and other dances that were derived in Europe. Bill "Bojangles" Robinson was the best of the black buck dancers, though he only became famous because he taught Shirley Temple (a little white girl movie star) to tap dance in her films. Blacks abandoned the so-called buck dance, like they did many of their natural talents, because whites did not approve of it. Buck dancing was vulgar, according to white people, so blacks strove hard to learn to waltz and do other so-called white dances. Yet Fred Astaire and Gene Kelly became very famous doing the buck dance and will probably go down in history as the greatest men who ever tap danced in America.

Jazz

The music played by the blacks for the white entertainment world was what whites wanted to hear. When black musicians played music that they liked, it was called jazz. Jazz is the only music whose origin is in America. Though this is definitely a fact, it will hardly go down in history as such. Jazz is mostly improvisation on the part of the musicians involved, which is ingenious in itself. Yet it is hardly accepted by the white establishment and even by many blacks, so it is not considered to be real classical music. Jazz has always been associated with drugs, dark rooms, and so-called "hepcat" blacks. Some black people condemned jazz early on because whites did not accept it. They spent much time trying to learn to understand so-called European classical music. This supposedly gave those blacks the status they thought they needed to be like white Americans. Blacks were unaware of the classical music played in India and Africa many, many years before Europeans ever played music.

A few black jazz musicians refused to abandon their style of music because of what people thought of it. Jazz musicians such as Miles Davis or Dizzy Gillespie could afford to continue to play jazz, so they did. Others had to conform to the establishment and play what they decided was music. Many black jazz players went broke and hungry, while others moved to Europe, where, strangely enough, jazz was accepted as an art form. Whites would not buy jazz albums, so jazz musicians became virtually extinct.

Though blacks had definitely been responsible for the entertainment of whites in America, they received little money for their display of talents. White men sponsored most of the concerts, bands, and groups and enjoyed most of the real profits that were made. Royalties were not dispersed properly if at all to the blacks for records and albums, and whites would steal their music and songs and make millions from them.

When black entertainers began to get wise to royalties and their value, whites decided to take over the music world. They took an uncoordinated truck driver with a guitar named Elvis Presley and decided to make him the king of rock and roll. They started placing music and groups in categories such as pop and rock and giving whites the credit for being the first. They made Bill Haley and his Comets the top rock group. They exploited such musicians as Chuck Berry, Chubby Checker, and Little Richard, copied them, and dropped them. After robbing them of their talents, they virtually wrote them out of history and decided that people like the Beatles, Presley, and the Rolling Stones were the music models for America. Like buck dancing, the kind of music blacks played and sung was not accepted by white people in general; therefore, blacks had to play and sing music like the whites or starve.

The blues was typical black music sung by lazy niggers, according to white people, and jitterbugging was definitely repulsive. Yet when a white singer can sing like a black, he makes more money than the average white singers or black singers, e.g., Tom Jones. Strangely enough, when a black singer can sing like whites, he can make more money, for the most part because he stands a better chance of being employed by whites. An example of a black singer who emulates whites is Johnny Mathis. In both cases, this is called crossing over. When a white can sing like a black, he can remain white and does not have to act black to remain popular and employed.

When a black can sing like a white, it is more profitable for him to act white, lose his identity, and be seen as little as possible with people of his own race. Because there is more money to be made by being black and singing white, this is the plateau that black singers and musicians attempt to reach. This way black culture is lost and black kids strive to sing and dance like white people rather than their own people.

High School

I felt no racial tension during my high school days, because everybody in my high school was black except for a handful of Indians. The few Indians were rather clannish, and we dark-complexioned blacks were used to lighter-skinned blacks receiving preferential treatment. Racism within the black race can be credited to the white men who raped black slave women and begot lighter African-Americans. The preferential treatment given to this lighter African-American followed the slaves into life after slavery. Being born into this way of thinking, I did not recognize the racism that took place in my high school.

Teachers and principals were lighter and had a tendency to treat the lighter-skinned students better. They were victims of the same way of thinking that I was and were not necessarily responsible for their actions. They themselves had received preferential treatment, this being the reason they were teachers and principals.

Many black schools of higher education requested a photograph when an application was submitted for admission to the school. Many of the students chosen to be admitted were chosen by the way they looked, and they were almost always light-skinned. At that time, light-skinned so-called good-looking blacks were pegged to go to college no matter how dumb they were. Darker-skinned blacks were considered only good for farm work, ditch digging, and cooking, no matter how smart or intelligent they were. The white man decided what an intelligent black should look like, so blacks determined intelligence among blacks in the same manner.

Whites accepted black preachers, no matter how dark they were, because all preachers were supposedly benevolent. This accounts for the fact that, in most black communities, the preacher was also the principal of the school and the spokesman for the community.

The only black men that would be accepted by blacks and whites and considered intelligent were the effeminate ones. The white men definitely preferred this type of black man over a real black masculine looking man, because he was not a threat to attract the white woman. Here again the white woman constituted the basis for racism toward the black man.

A dark-complexioned black with kinky hair would be scrutinized and highly questioned by blacks and whites as to his intelligence and qualifications before being accepted for a position. His character had to be impeccable, and he would constantly be under pressure to perform on a high level. On the other hand, a tall, light-skinned black would be accepted readily by blacks and whites with little or no examination.

Big black men have always been a threat to white men because of the possibility of their becoming unruly.

Blacks did not see the wrong in such discrimination within the race, because it had always been that way.

In retrospect, our being all of the same race in my high school helped blacks tremendously. The teachers, though they were mostly light-skinned, were all black and showed concern for each student. Every teacher was like a member of every student's family and would visit the student's home sometimes during the school year. The students had the uttermost respect for and faith in the teachers and felt free to present their everyday problems to them. This personal concern and guidance often followed the student throughout life.

Not only did I not learn about racism in high school, but I also did not learn about black people. The white board of education designated the first week in February Black History Week. I never knew if this week was observed by white students in their schools. I also didn't know why black people allowed men from another race to decide what, when, and how long they should commemorate the history of their own people.

Unfortunately, black children learned more American and European history than we did black history in high school. These courses were required in all schools, whereas black history courses were not required even in black high schools.

Black people did not know that the white people who financed their schools also decided what their curricula would be. Blacks did not finance nor did they seek to finance their own institutions of learning. Their ultimate goal was to find a white donor or sponsor who would "pay the piper and call the tune."

Black students were the last concern of a people who was striving to be like another race.

The few black heroes we were allowed to commemorate during Black History Week were the ones that whites decided were heroes. Famous blacks who spoke out against racism or fought and died for freedom (Marcus Garvey, Nat Turner, and others) were seldom, if ever, mentioned during this week. White school boards controlled Black History Week just as they did everything else in the segregated black schools. Some black children thought of Black History Week as a time to recite black speeches and act in plays by and/or about blacks. They were not motivated to associate the history of the black people they were portraying with themselves. Like many of the other holidays celebrated in America (such as Christmas and Easter), the significance of Black History Week was lost in most black schools.

Being in an all-black school was beneficiary, because most of the students were of the same economic background. Here a student's financial status did not determine the attention he or she would receive in a classroom or elsewhere.

All of the students were black; therefore, the stars were not picked according to race, but strictly according to performance. Black athletes competed hard against each other and had no problem with the best man winning. Very few players were on the team or teams because of who they or their fathers were. The best of the athletes received scholarships to the best black colleges, where they were encouraged by black instructors to do their best athletically and academically. White colleges, athletes, records, and performances were not problems for the black athletes to reckon with, because blacks could not attend most of the white colleges anyway. Black coaches didn't have to worry about coaching at a white college for the same reason. Coaches and players performed at their peak and were happy where they were.

The Woodyard

I have written about the sawmill where we obtained om wood. I did not mention anything about the woodyard where we took the wood, cut it up, and prepared it to be sold. People would buy strips and slabs of wood from us to be used in their stoves for cooking and fireplaces for heating. I guess it is fair to say this was Daddy's profession. This was our livelihood.

I did not learn about racism in the woodyard because Daddy was my boss and all of the boys who worked for him were black. Ninety percent of the people who bought wood from us were black. The white people who bought wood from us had no real significance or impact on my life, because they were in charge and they came to us. With our income coming from the black community, I came in direct contact with very few whites and did not learn how I was supposed to act around them, as did black people who had to work for whites directly.

Having our own business had it advantages during that time, in spite of the kind of work it was. White people in Clinton did not consider the lumberyard to be a profitable business; therefore, they didn't watch Daddy very closely until he bought a new 1947 truck. The white policemen began stopping him regularly and searching the truck for "white lightning." They were sure Daddy must be engaging in some kind of illegal activity if he was able to buy a new truck and have a car also. Daddy sold the car and kept the truck, but the harassment continued. The white people in authority could not believe they had allowed a black man to get by them and make more money than they meant for him to make. A black businessman was forced to keep a low profile if he wanted to remain in business. I did not know that a black man's income often was controlled and monitored strictly by the white establishment in America. White men have always known that few white women would choose a poor black man over a prosperous white man. Here we have the problem of the white woman and racism.

The Church

I did not learn about racism in my church, because everybody in the church I belonged to was black. There were two First Baptist Churches in the small town of Clinton, the black one located at 900 College Street and the white one located at 400 College Street. The black First Baptist Church was opened to all, and when a white man came to our church he was invited down front and given a seat near the altar. The white First Baptist Church, located just a few blocks up the street from the black First Baptist Church, was closed to blacks, and when a black man came to their church they would ask him what he wanted and hurry him on his way. If he came to worship, he would be directed to the black First Baptist

Church. I did not question that kind of religion it was that condoned such double standards, because it had always been that way. Blacks did not question how whites could preach about love and kindness to mankind and turn a man away from the house where they preached it. I never understood how God supposedly condoned segregated churches when both the churches' missions were supposed to have been the same. Such love for your fellowman never seemed to have manifested itself when it came to integration with the white Christians. Black Americans have been conditioned to love their greatest enemy, which obviously is the white man.

I never understood why blacks could read a book that was written by and about a race of people many of whom are definitely racists and decide it was written for them also. In spite of the fact that almost everything written in the Bible took place in or around Africa, black people neither know, care, nor question whether the Bible should have been about people of color rather than about whites. As a matter of fact, blacks are often confronted with the question of whether there were any blacks mentioned in the Bible or not. Being ignorant of the Bible's geographical setting, most blacks' answer is no.

Very few blacks know anything about or question the origin of their religion. They are unaware of the fact that Christianity began in Africa many, many years before the white man adopted it. Black people don't consider the fact that they should study extensively anything that promises them eternal life to be sure that is, in fact, what is happening.

During the time of slavery, white men who allowed blacks to become Christians were not considered racists when they would not allow slaves to worship together with them. White church people had no problem making blacks worship from the back of the church with a high partition between them and the blacks. Black people who have accepted a white Jesus and Christianity have remained more reverent and dedicated than many of the white people who gave them the religion. White people must feel superior to black people by the mere fact that they have a God in their own image. I am of the opinion that racist white people would not worship a God that was not in their own image, especially if the God were black. Many blacks are satisfied that they will someday be angels in heaven, though it is impossible for them to visualize a black angel in heaven or any other place. They have been thoroughly brainwashed into worshipping a God who is not of their own image. All of the Gods worshipped by our African forefathers were of our own image. Black Americans would not think of having faith in a black God or a black angel flying in heaven. The realization of this fact is frightening when you consider how many black minds are controlled by religion in America.

I had no idea that I was a potential victim of such brainwashing when I was forced to attend Sunday school, church, and the BTU (Baptist Training Union) without question. My parents did not browbeat me with religious indoctrination, but we were like the average black family who thought that almost everything that was fun was a sin. We were like most God-fearing black families who felt God would make it right for black people someday. When it came to white people who seemed to have everything, though they were racist and evil, my mother would say, "Don't worry, son; they'll get theirs." Of course my question was "When?"

Chapter 26

North Carolina College for Negroes

I was faced with segregation immediately after I arrived at North Carolina College for Negroes in Durham, North Carolina. Although this was an all-black school, racism among the students and faculty ran rampant. I realized immediately that my dark complexion was a negative factor, because I was watching the groups and gatherings. I was watching the students that were being chosen to be in charge and the trend of the instructors. Most of all, I could tell by the way I was being treated by the other students.

I was born knowing that dark-complexioned blacks were at the bottom of the totem pole in America. This had been true even in my neighborhood, but it had not been a problem, because it had always been that way and was all I knew. Now, for the first time, I was witnessing racism within the black race, and it was open and blatant. I had been pushed back before because of the color of my skin, but it didn't really matter, because I was still popular in high school and rewarded reasonably well, I thought, for my achievements.

I sang in the college choir with several tenors whose voices were not as good as or as trained as my voice was. Hyton Williams was apparently chosen to be the soloist over me because of the color of his skin and his light eyes and straight hair. I accepted his being chosen over me at first, knowing there were enough solos to go around. I also felt that in time my college would discover and acknowledge the fact that my voice was better. I became rather paranoid, however, when I was faced with the fact of not being accepted by my college as a lyric tenor. When Hyton and I did the same solo, he would receive thunderous applause, especially from the female choir members. I would receive only a little applause.

As I stated previously, I had been very popular in high school, especially with the women. I could barely get into a conversation with the women on the college campus. I watched this situation very closely and tried to maintain my composure and positive self-image. I learned it was unpopular for a woman to identify herself with those whom society had condemned. Dark-complexioned women who identified with dark-complexioned men were condemning themselves to apparent doom, because society had already demanded that they match themselves with light-skinned men. This was mandated for them many years ago for the possible babies' sake. Many of the women at college expected to leave there with husbands. They knew their parents would not approve of their returning home with dark-complexioned, kinky-haired men, no matter how intelligent the man was. While the dark-complexioned male students would have preferred lighter-skinned women, they would pair off with a female of any color for companionship. While this situation was as ludicrous as it sounds, it was disheartening to be almost completely ostracized by your peers merely because of your color.

The male students treated dark-complexioned fellows almost the same as the female students treated them. The light-skinned "pretty boys" ran around together and of course attracted the so-called pretty girls. Most of the fellows were rather congenial in the dormitory or on the athletic field. On the open campus, however, they couldn't risk being ranked with the so-called unwanted. Mr. Handly, the black science teacher, avoided calling on the very dark-complexioned students in the classroom when at all possible. On occasions when he finally recognized one of our raised hands, he would reluctantly accept our comment and move on. I tried to ignore this fact also until he chose all of the light skinned women to work in the laboratory and grade our test papers. This discrimination became more obvious when we received our final grades and discovered the dumbest of the light skinned students received As and Bs while the dark-skinned students received Cs, Ds, and Fs. Mr. Handly's wife was as white as any white woman, and he chose his associates very carefully. He apparently had no idea how he was ruining the lives of blacks and wasting their minds. Unfortunately, because of black-onblack racism, I thought less of myself while I was in college than ever before. Being rejected by my own people, I felt helpless and worthless, with nowhere really to turn.

I had to live off campus my sophomore year, because Daddy could not afford to have me and my sister on campus at the same time. Not only had I learned about racism during those two school years, I had also experienced being hungry, with no food available most of the time. I had always gotten a haircut every two weeks, whether I needed one or not. When I received my monthly allowance of five dollars from Daddy, at least one dollar was for food. Invariably I would get one haircut a month and be paranoid the last half of the month with my woolly head. My hair really was not that long and woolly, because it didn't grow that fast. I had been programmed to think that when two weeks had passed, my head looked unpresentable. When a man was dark-complexioned and kinky-headed, society demanded that he at least kept a close-cut haircut. I had a choice of being hungry or getting a haircut during the middle of each month while I was in school. The hunger drive won every month, because I had never before been that hungry and without means to obtain food in my entire life. During the summer after my sophomore year in college, I was faced with several problems. I had become disgruntled with school for many reasons and had no real desire to return there in September. Most of all, my social life had been very limited and my ego was at rock bottom. Though I had cultivated friendships with several of the male students, I had been virtually ignored by the majority of the female students. I felt a great need to do something different with my life.

Chapter 27
Me and Uncle Sam

I decided for several reasons, to go to the local draft board and tell them I was ready to be inducted into the military service. In doing so, my name would be moved up on the list and I would be in the next group leaving Clinton for the service. The biggest reason I made this decision was because I knew Daddy could no longer afford to send me and my sister to college at the same time. I definitely did not want to spend another year in college hungry. Most black men entered the military service because of economic reasons. I also was motivated to make this decision after I was hired as an orderly at the local hospital and sent immediately to the outside of the hospital to pull weeds. I didn't think they would have hired a white man who had completed his sophomore year in college to pull weeds around the hospital. Another big reason I decided to go into the service was to be able to send Mother an allotment so she would not have to continue to slave in Dr. Johnson's kitchen.

I had already passed the physical exam for the military service and had been exempted because I was in school. Shortly after they moved my name up on the list, I received my "Greetings from Uncle Sam."

As ordered by my draft notice, I met the army recruiting bus in front of the A and P grocery store at nine o'clock one morning. Mother accompanied me to the bus and, I learned later, cried until the bus was out of sight. Somehow going away to school had not been like this departing. I felt a sort of emptiness. I felt as if I were going to fight a war all by myself.

This was in 1951 and, unbeknownst to me, President Truman had signed a bill in 1945 declaring the United States Armed Forces to be integrated.

I don't know why I had never thought of whether the military was segregated or not. Everything else in America was, and I was used to it being that way. It also did not occur to me that I was being inducted into the army of the country in which I was considered a second-class citizen.

We arrived in Fayetteville, North Carolina, about forty-five minutes after leaving Clinton. We said the "Pledge of Allegiance" late in the afternoon, and it was announced that we were officially soldiers in the U.S. Army. I remember the tightness I had in my chest for fear I might have been turned down for some last-minute reason. I also can remember feeling somewhat patriotic for the first time in my life. Also, for the first time it seemed the flag had some significance to me.

All of this had taken place at the induction station at Fort Bragg. For whatever reason, this station was located in town. We were advised by our white bus driver, who was not in the military, to take care of our needs before boarding the bus. He said he would be driving us to Fort Jackson in South Carolina and he would not be stopping along the way for anything. He told us there was no bathroom on the bus. He suggested to the white inductees that they go inside the bus station next door to relieve themelves and purchase food.

Like most of the public facilities in America, the bathrooms in the bus station were segregated. As a matter of fact, the bus station was segregated, so that the black soldiers were not allowed to use the bathroom in the station. We also could not enter the station to purchase food. All of the public facilities in Fayetteville were segregated, so we black soldiers did as we had always done. We went behind the building to relieve ourselves and bought food through the little hole cut in the window at the bus station. Of course, they waited on all of the white soldiers before they waited on any of the black soldiers.

We all waited patiently at the hole, however, because that was what we were accustomed to.

We black soldiers also had to ride in the back of the bus on the way to Fort Jackson, because integration, even on an army bus, was against the law. Even though the army was supposedly integrated, soldiers had to obey the civilian laws when they were not on the army post.

At Fort Jackson we were given our initial issue of clothing and other gear needed for basic training. We also took all kinds of physical and mental examinations. I apparently scored rather high on the exams, because I received positive responses from some of the instructors who were testing us. These tests determined where the new inductees would be transferred for basic training. After about a week, I was sent from Fort Jackson to Camp Gordon, Georgia. This was a military signal corps camp in Augusta, Georgia.

One of the first things I noticed about the company I was assigned to was there were only three blacks in the company of three hundred men. They were supposed to have been slowly integrating each company, with the greatest of care not to put too many blacks in one company. It was also apparent that the average white in the company had a high school education while the blacks had all been to college.

Regardless of the circumstances, I had planned to do well, as most blacks do when they enter a new situation. Shortly after my joining the army, it became obvious that none of the blacks was in a position to advance. All of the squad leaders chosen were white, and the cadre acted as though we blacks in the company were invisible.

Basic Training

My eight weeks of basic training were like one long nightmare. The rugged mental and physical training posed no problem for me, because my toil in Daddy's woodyard and life in general had taught me to be tough. The problems stemmed from the fact that our company was poorly managed by a "ninety-day wonder" (a young white second lieutenant with ninety days of training at an officers training school) and a first sergeant who had been in the service for forty-one years. The first sergeant showed no respect whatsoever for the lieutenant and ran the company like it was his family. This sounds good, but did not work, because the cadrymen in charge were dumb and prejudiced.

The cooks weren't only racist; they were also alcoholics. Two of them were so-called rednecks from the Deep South, and the other two were big, dumb Indians. This is not to say, by any means, that Indians are dumb. These two were, however, and what's worse, they seemed to have been under the spell or command of the two rednecks, especially when they were drinking. Both the cadrymen were rednecks also. One thing I was learning was that white people didn't know as much about blacks as we knew about them. Many of them had never really had any dealings with blacks and everything they knew about us was what they had heard or read. There were few, if any, televisions around, because they were new on the market and expensive. The only black television show was "Amos and Andy." The cooks, cadrymen, and white soldiers in the company were surprised to learn that the blacks could think rationally and make intelligent decisions. Many of the soldiers made it their business to be friendly. However, some of them treated us like the second-class citizens they felt we were. Unfortunately, that seemed to have been the way the cooks and cadrymen felt toward us, because that is the way they treated us.

I might note here that one of the three so-called blacks in the company was actually a Puerto Rican. His brother, who was also in the company, was considered white and treated white by those in charge because he looked white. One evening we were all on the bus leaving the army post. Being in the segregated state of Georgia, when we were off the army post the bus driver would stop the bus and the black soldiers would have to move to the back of the bus. The driver on this occasion told the darker Puerto Rican soldier to move to the back of the bus and his brother attempted to accompany him. The bus driver threatened to call the police if the so-called white brother insisted upon going to the back of the bus with his brother. The driver insisted that the so-called white brother was white and reminded him that integration was against the law whether they were brothers or not. This was the first of my knowing that whites could not integrate with blacks. I had thought all along that the integration laws only pertained to black people. I always felt if a white man wanted to drink from a water fountain marked Colored Only, he could do so. I knew, of course, that blacks would be arrested for drinking from a water fountain marked Whites Only.

When we blacks rode into Augusta with our Italian friend, we would have to hide on the floor of his car. We would sneak out of his car as he entered the black section of town when no policeman was in sight. If we had gotten caught in the car with our white friend, we would have all been arrested for "integrating."

The cooks and cadrymen had private rooms upstairs and downstairs at the front of the barracks. Their wishes were the troops' command, no matter how ludicrous or what time of day or night it was. They would drink liquor daily, sometimes all day, and harass the troops. The cooks, being in charge of the kitchen and food, had an added measure of control. Most of the time the first sergeant had no idea what was going on in the company, and he called the cooks and the cadrymen his boys. Needless to say, the troops were at his boys' mercy.

On weekends the troops would wait for the drunks to return to the company, like wives who wait for their drunken husbands to come home Saturday night.

Chief, as the big Indian was called, and his crew would return to the company on Friday and Saturday night and do anything they felt like doing. Most of the white soldiers could afford to go to a motel or elsewhere on weekends. I could neither afford to do that nor did I like the idea of being afraid to stay in a place where I was supposed to be safe and feel at home.

The cadrymen, cooks, and Chief would consume bottle after bottle of liquor on weekends. They would get drunk and loud and defy anyone to even act as though they didn't like what they did. The cadrymen and cooks took advantage of Chief's ignorance and brute physical strength. If they told him to kick a door down, he would obey them and they would all laugh hilariously. Basic trainees were considered "peons" with no rights. Even if we had any rights, we were unaware of them and afraid to ask. We were new to the company and to the army, and for all we knew, this went on in all companies all of the time. We were outranked by everyone, and as I stated before, the cooks controlled the food.

I was the only black among fifty trainees in the upstairs of the barracks. Moses was the only black downstairs. Moses had married his childhood sweetheart before joining the army and was happy to be in the service, earning a steady income.

One Saturday evening, I returned to the company at midnight after I had seen enough of the black soldiers downtown drooling over those scroungy-looking old Georgian women. Moses met me at the door of the barracks and said, "Man, you don't want to go upstairs." When l asked him why not, he said, "Cause Chief and them are on the warpath up there." I could hear what sounded like bottles being bowled up the aisle upstairs. I recognized the voices, and the drunken laughter was nothing new for a weekend in our company.

I remained downstairs until I became too sleepy to care. I decided I was going to bed in spite of what was happening upstairs.

When I reached the top of the stairs, the first thing that could be seen was the broken glass in the aisle from the empty liquor bottles that had been bowled after they were emptied. All of the footlockers and bunks had been turned over, and the big four were sitting at the far end of the barracks on the floor, singing. I was frightened stiff as I moved slowly toward my bunk bed. They ignored me completely, however, and to my surprise, my locker and bed were the only ones on the floor that had not been overturned. I quietly pulled off my clothes and went to bed.

I was still shaking and wondering why they had not bothered me. I also wondered what I would have done had my bunk and locker been overturned. They were apparently so drunk that they didn't even see me.

I was finding it very difficult to get to sleep, because the lights were still on, even though it was past 1:00 A.M. I had not dared turn them off when I came upstairs.

I was shocked when I heard someone downstairs yell, "Attention!" This meant that someone had the nerve to call the officer of the day (OD) on Chief and his crew or the OD had seen the lights on after hours. I couldn't wait for him to come upstairs and see the mess the big four had made. I was sure he would haul the four of them away to the stockade.

Chief and company also had heard the order downstairs and were well aware there was an officer downstairs. As a matter of fact, they were laughing and mimicking the officer and the driver before they came upstairs. When they came upstairs and the driver yelled "Attention," I did not move, because I had already decided to remain in bed and fake being asleep. I was peeking from under the sheets and could see the comical sight of the four drunks standing in attention at the end of the barracks, saluting the officer. The astonishing fact, however, was, the captain said, "As you were, men" and he and his driver cut the lights out and departed. The lights were back on before the OD got out of the building, and the fun and laughter were louder than ever.

For some reason, I decided something had to be done. I did not consider the fact that I was not the likely person to take on the fight, because Chief and his friends had not bothered me. Nevertheless, that Monday evening while the others were cleaning up their area, I decided to request to see the sergeant. The sergeant, who was sixty-nine years old, was irritable that morning because he had not been well enough to bowl with his bowling team. He cut me real short when I told him what had been happening on weekends and what had happened this particular weekend. He said, "Oh, them boys were just having a little fun, don't pay 'em no mind."

I was well aware that Chief and his raiders were home free. Now the question "Why me?" loomed larger than ever. I felt that any moment the sergeant would be telling Chief that I had told on them.

That Monday night I was reminded that what the cooks and cadrymen did was not my business. I was awakened in the middle of the night by a scrawny little redneck cook who had apparently been to the beer hall and gotten drunk. He was standing at the end of the barracks near his room, clad in his underwear and T-shirt. He was swinging a ferocious-looking machete from side to side. When I had awakened enough to realize what he was up to, it was apparent he was talking to me. He said, "The yellow-bellied nigger better not raise his head or I'll cut it off." I had barely peeked from under my sheets when suddenly I realized I was a prisoner in my own bed. I was sweating and scared, shaking and cold. My heart seemed to be beating so loud and heavy that I held my chest in an effort to quieten it down for fear he would hear it. I could not figure out why this particular cook was so hostile, but I knew he didn't like me, because he had always looked at me as though I were slime. He seemed to hate me simply because I was there. This time it was obvious he was angry because I had gone to the sergeant about his weekend escapades. The sergeant had squealed. I wondered what he had told the cook and his buddies. Would they all be after me? Anything he had said to them amounted to a tap on the wrist, if, in fact, he had reprimanded them at all.

It occurred to me as I was lying there, scared to breathe, that I had never really been afraid of a white man before. I had heard what I was supposed to do to a white man or anyone else who called me "Nigger." Now I'd been called a "black son of a bitch," and none of what I had heard I was supposed to do made sense at that particular moment. In fact, I had heard the words black and nigger on several occasions since I had been in Georgia, but they had not been directed to me. Now these words were being yelled directly at me in a life-or-death situation and I felt like a coward because I chose to live. The cook said he would cut me from "asshole to elbows." I knew I could win in a fair fight. I also knew I could not beat him with that machete in his hand. If I won, I lost anyway, because he was a cook, with the cadrymen and the other cooks on his side. The food was bad, but it was food and better than no food at all.

While lying there silently, I became aware of how very quiet it was upstairs and that this cook was the only one talking. I wondered why at least one of the other fellows did not rise up in my defense. Most of the fellows upstairs claimed to be my friends, saying that they liked Negroes and, of course, "some of their best friends were Negroes." None of them bothered defending me that night.

The cook's vocabulary was obviously very limited, and I suppose he was tired of yelling the same threats and obscenities to no avail. I was cowardly, remaining under my cover, and wasn't about to oblige him by moving a hair. When he stopped yelling and returned to his room, I was still lying quietly in the same cold, wet spot. I needed desperately to go to the bathroom, to do all of the things you do when you are scared to death. but I didn't dare move. I was glad there were no other blacks upstairs for me to face the next morning. Somehow I didn't quite mind appearing to be a coward in front of the white fellows. I didn't feel I would lose any prestige among them. They too had acted cowardly by not intervening in some way. I would have had to fight if there had been other blacks upstairs.

I was still wide awake when the bugle sounded for reveille. I didn't know exactly how much basic training I was getting in Georgia, but I certainly knew I was getting a profound lesson in racism.

The first time I raised my head that morning, I saw the new little redneck sergeant, fresh from Korea, who had joined the cadrymen standing in the same spot where my assailant had stood a few hours before. He turned the lights on as he had been doing in the morning since he had arrived at the base and said, "All right, let's hit it." Immediately, some of the men upstairs who had made friends with the sergeant asked what had happened to him and why he had not met them in town, as he had promised. He said, "I was right down there by that nigger theater waiting for y'all." I had been very slow that morning after having been so frightened and not having slept during the night. At that moment, I was making my bed and licking my wounds. When I heard the word nigger, again, I was too weak to fight. It occurred to me I could be fighting every other day about those words, because they seemed to have been used down there in Georgia at random.

I was nineteen years old and wanted to live. I had planned to "lose my identity" in that white company, yet still do my best to excel. That morning, however, I was well aware of my race, color, and identity. I was faced with the problem of trying to be black, in a white company, with dignity.

I didn't eat breakfast and ate lunch only because I was hungry and beginning to get weak. On the way to the company that evening, the little sergeant yelled, "Catch up the line, soldier." I was the shortest person in the formation; therefore, I was in the very back of the formation. I was weary and did not feel like keeping in step in the vigorous manner required. When he told me to catch up the line for the second time, I quietly and politely stepped out of the formation and continued to walk on the sidewalk. The sergeant said, "Get back in that formation, soldier," and I ignored him. They went on to the company without me. I had no idea what would or could happen to me. Frankly, I didn't care. I was fed up and could not take any more at that moment. I arrived at the company about five minutes after the troops had arrived. The little sergeant met me as soon as I entered the company area. He said, "What's wrong, Faison? You sick?" I said, "No" and kept walking. I had decided to do what I had done, so I would not let him give me an excuse for doing it. I felt I had already let myself and my people down and somehow had to register a protest, for them and for my own sanity. I never encountered a problem with the sergeant or the cook again.

The bathroom was located next door to the toilet, where six white fellows were enjoying their after-meal crap game and chewing the fat. None of them was aware that I was shaving within hearing range of them. One of them asked my white friend Mullens what the novel he was reading was about. Mullen said, "Oh, it's about this nigger washwoman fucking all the white men she could." They all laughed and a couple of them asked to see the book after he finished with it. They were still telling black jokes when Mullens came out of the toilet into the bathroom. His face was flushed when he began to apologize to me. He told me he was brought up in a small town in Oklahoma where everybody referred to blacks as niggers.

He asked me to forgive him. While I felt he was sincere, I was learning not to trust white people. He was the first white person I had ever referred to as my friend anyway. We had befriended each other because of our mutual love of jazz. It seemed one on one; white people were all right and treated me as though I was a human being. When they were together, however, many were like different people and definitely white.

I breezed through the radio operators' school with few if any racial incidents. I had more black soldiers to interact with, which made living in Georgia more bearable. For many of us, this was the first time we had had a chance to be with white people. For some this was prestigious, and they sought the company of whites at all times. I, for one, realized early that "birds of a feather flock together." I watched whites tolerating the company blacks. I did not want to be tolerated or accommodated just for the sake of rubbing shoulders with whites. The association could only exist on the army post anyway. It seemed to me to be ludicrous to have a friend on the post that you could not associate with in society.

Prior to our graduation and before the Korean War ended, all black soldiers' orders were marked FECOM. This meant they were going to Korea, where the war was actually being fought. This was a standard joke among the black soldiers around graduation time, because at that time the graduates received orders for new assignments. These black men had no idea at the time that the joke was on them.

Blacks had fought bravely in every war in which America had been involved. They were reluctantly placed on the front lines and on strategic assignments during the two world wars because the so-called prestigious positions were reserved for the red-blooded white American males. Whites did not feel that blacks should be dying for this country, because they did not really feel that blacks belonged in this country. It was supposedly an honor to give your life for your country. In spite of the hard times blacks had prior to the world wars or any of the wars in which America became involved, they were still anxious to defend their country.

By the time the Korean War came about, many young white men were no longer so brave to give their lives for their country. Besides that, they were fully aware of this unwanted black human being who needed to be in the military and wanted to fight for this country. They were beginning to realize that when a black died on the front line or wherever, it was one less black they had to worry about. Blacks needed the financial security offered by the military, and apparently that undying patriotism that the founding fathers had felt was gone forever.

Blacks were being sent to the front lines daily during the Korean War, so naturally more blacks were losing their lives on the front lines than men of any other race involved on the American side.

It had not occurred to me that the war was virtually over when I graduated from radio operators school; therefore I was satisfied that my orders would read FECOM (Far East Command). When my name was called and the sergeant read EUCOM (Europe Command), I, along with the others in the company, was flabbergasted. Never in my wildest dreams did I think I would ever be going to Germany.

Looking Back

Riding the bus (Trailways or Greyhound) to go home on holidays was a horrible experience for blacks. At that time, most people, especially blacks, could only afford to ride a bus when they took a trip. You could hardly get near a bus station in an army town during a holiday. Schoolchildren and low- and middleincome white people also rode the bus on holidays. Blacks were in the back of the ticket lines, in the back of the line when the bus was loading, and in the back of the bus (the last four seats). During holidays, only the long backseat by the bathroom was left for blacks if there were whites without seats. If there was one white without a seat, both blacks in a seat would have to stand and the white person would occupy the whole seat alone. If there were seats available in the front of the bus and blacks standing because their four designated seats were full, the driver would not ask whites to move up and allow blacks to sit in the next seats. Blacks also could not go to the empty seats up front.

They would have to stand, no matter how far they were going and even if the line was to the front door. When a black had to stand in the aisle next to a white person who was sitting, he or she had to be careful not to touch or lean on the white person, no matter how rough the ride was or how sharp the curves were. Blacks, especially the men, were obliged to keep their eyes straight ahead, because white women did not have to tolerate being stared at by these people. Many would stare back at you as if you were the scum of the earth. The threat of you being put off the bus was forever present, because if a black man accidently insulted a white, this would be grounds enough for the black man to be removed bodily from the bus. The temperament of the bus driver determined how blacks would be treated on a trip. We had to be able to read the driver and act accordingly. Some drivers would begin threatening blacks before they entered the bus, making them fear not being allowed to get on the bus. For no reason at all a driver could refuse to let a passenger get on the bus. This was nerve-racking for blacks because they were at the mercy of the driver and no drivers seemed to care for them.

My happiest day was the day I left Georgia. Several of us hailed a cab with the idea of sharing the expense among us. The driver was black and talkative. All of the passengers were black, and the subject was getting away from white folks in Georgia. The driver was very vocal on the subject until we reached the station. I noticed the expression on his face changed and he was quiet. By the time he came to a stop at the bus station, I noticed a white cabdriver coming toward our cab. Before he snatched the door of our cab open, our driver jumped out of the cab and apparently was ready for whatever was to take place. I was sure he could handle the situation by the way he had been talking in the cab prior to the incident. To my surprise, our driver began "Uncle Tomming" and tap-dancing before he was out of the cab. It seemed white cabdrivers had total jurisdiction over the cab fares at the bus station. Our cabdriver continued to assure the white cabdriver he would not be picking up a fare at the station. Such grinning and scratching I had not seen since I had been in Georgia. I knew things were not much better for blacks anyplace else in America, but I certainly was glad to get out of Georgia.

Overseas Duty

The eight days on the water were a new experience for me, because I had never lived near any water and, being relatively poor, we could not afford to go to places where there was water very often.

There was a feeling in the air that was rather difficult to describe—a feeling of comradeship, all for one and one for all, surprisingly there among all of the ship's occupants. Almost all of us were going away to a strange faraway place, and the fact that the war was not being fought in Euro pe had no relevance at that time. Men have a tendency to get together and do very well when there are no women around. They have nothing to prove to each other for the most part and no one to show off for. When there is a common interest among men only, they spend less time competing and more time doing the best job that can be done. Unfortunately, African-American men have been programmed to try harder and do their best no matter what the situation. In this particular case, the white soldiers could relax because there were no white women around for them to keep away from the black soldiers. We were all like brothers on our way to perform a service for our country.

Things changed rapidly, however, as soon as the ship landed in Bremerhaven. There were a few enlisted women at the port of debarkation, and of course the European women were white.

Racism was immediately apparent. The two black enlisted women there were in popular demand. The black soldiers wanted them, the American white soldiers wanted them, the German soldiers wanted them, and the Armenian soldiers wanted them. Unlike women of other races, the black Wacs totally ignored the black soldiers. They barely looked at us, but acted as though we were invisible. I'm sure that past experience had taught them that the black soldiers had less money than any of the white soldiers. Unfortunately, many blacks had never learned to love, respect, and identify with members of their own race. On the contrary, black women were taught from the time they were brought up by all in charge to stay away from a "nigger" if at all possible.

The white enlisted women were considered to be the "cream of the crop" in Europe, as they were all over the world at that time. They too had the pick of the litter and shunned the black soldiers. They knew that all they could get from a black soldier was love, promises, and lies. White enlisted women seldom if ever wasted their time dating a black enlisted man.

The white soldiers were on the job again, making sure that the white women gave none of their time and attention to the black soldiers. Their job now was twofold in that they had to watch the white American women and the white German women. In Germany, if either of these women associated with the black American soldiers, she was ostracized by white society. They were ridiculed by the white soldiers and German women and labeled nigger lovers by both parties. This would force any German woman that associated with a black soldier to the lower-class section of the city where blacks were also forced to frequent.

Financial differences, racism, and even segregation had found their way to Europe, if in fact they were not already there. I would like to attribute this to the fact that the white soldier had been there during World War II. but Hitler had preached racism even before the war began. The true Germans did not appreciate the white soldiers' being there any more than they did the black soldiers.

The "brown babies" and the mothers of these children were catching hell from everyone. Being the offspring of an American soldier was bad enough. Being the offspring of a black American soldier was a "fate worse than death" in Germany. The war had ended just seven years prior to our arriving in Germany. These children were entering their teens, and because of their color and visibility they were nothing but reminders to the Germans of a war that had been lost by their country.

Most of the mothers of the "brown babies" had been prostitutes during the war. The white German society made them continue to be prostitutes, even though they were much older and tired of being in the streets. Many of them were forced to hide the fact that they were the mothers of a brown baby in order to obtain a job and earn a decent living. These who had to remain in the streets proudly proclaimed that as long as they had their bodies, their "brown babies" would never suffer from the lack of food.

Black soldiers found themselves in the same bag the y had been in at home in America. White soldiers filled most of the high ranks, and the blacks who achieved high ranks had in many cases certainly tap-danced and sold their souls to get there.

My friend Moses and I were called in by the lieutenant in charge of our detachment for a briefing. We were reminded that we were the first black s to be assigned to the Twenty-second Signal Detachment. The lieutenant assured us that if we were good boys, other blacks would be assigned to our detachment. Like most "first blacks," we were happy to be first and promised to be good for the sake of the future. As in basic training, we were like specimens who were watched to see if we really were like other human beings. Moses apparently had no problem with this and lost his black identity right away. I struggled hard to keep my black identity, only to discover that we blacks really had never had an identity in America. During and after slavery we were obliged to imitate white America to the point that few, if any, of us knew any other way to act. I acted white for a very short while until I missed being black and realized, after a few rude awakenings, that I would always be black.

As for associating and mingling with whites in the company area, things were fine. The problems stemmed from outside this area, where there were so-called white bars and black bars, white areas and black areas. When the blacks' and whites' paths crossed, there were racial problems and fights, just like in America.

Prior to my going to Europe, I had heard of whites going abroad to Europe. Blacks loved to imitate whites and travel to Europe, not realizing that white Americans' forefathers had come from Europe. Many white Europeans were no fonder of black American soldiers than whites in America were. I learned while in Europe that white people were white people, all over the world, and their opinion toward blacks often was the same.

Back in the States

When we soldiers woke up at the harbor in New York, that strange feeling of comradeship was no longer present. Whites seemed to have drifted to one side of the ship and blacks to the other. All of the plans my white friends and I had made to stay in touch and visit each other had dissolved. The message to the black soldiers was loud and clear. We were back in America, where segregation was still alive and well. I could virtually feel the blanket of segregation cover my body.

The experience I had received as a radio operator (International Morse Code) and in teletype and tape delay was no help to me in civilian life. There were no blacks being hired in this line of work. The fact that I was certified by the United States government had no bearing on the hiring practices in America in 1953.

I returned to North Carolina College after I was discharged from the army to become a teacher, preacher, doctor or lawyer. Those were the professions designated for blacks, though hopes of achieving success in the latter two were very farfetched. There were a few exceptions, but many of the southern schools did not encourage the black students, especially if they intended to remain in the South.

I had no real aspiration to return to NCC, even though its name had been changed from North Carolina College for Negroes to North Carolina College at Durham.

I returned just in time to be a part of a very famous assembly in the B. N. Duke Auditorium. Dr. Alphonso Elder called the entire student body to the auditorium during the lunch hour to announce the passing of the 1954 school-integration decision (Brown versus Ferguson-The Board of Education of Topeka, Kansas). The loud burst of applause indicated to me that the majority of the student body knew what he was talking about. Of course, I had been out of the country and the army newspaper (Stars and Stripes) had carried little or no news about civil rights. Striking down the separate but equal doctrine was supposedly the beginning of true integration into American society for black Americans. With equal educational opportunities, we felt we were on our way.

Chapter 28
The Sixties

The struggle for equality and parity among the races really caught on during the sixties. Nothing was gained by blacks without a lot of blood, sweat, and tears, in spite of the passing of the school-integration decision. Blacks were marching all over America singing "We Shall Overcome."

Black leaders like Jesse Jackson, Dick Gregory, Martin Luther King, Jr., and Malcolm X were speaking to enthusiastic audiences of mostly black students. Though many of the black churches were used for preparing blacks for protests, the growing concern for whites was the fact that black college campuses were becoming the training grounds for protests. White people knew that black church people have never been a real threat to commit violence, but the benevolent black church people finally seemed to be waking up.

Black students were uniting and saying, "I'm black and I'm proud" at their sit-ins and marches. Intelligent, energetic, fed-up blacks like Stokely Carnlichael and Angela Davis were becoming a threat to the white power structure.

Blacks spent the next few years struggling to integrate white schools. Few, if any, whites rushed to integrate black schools. Instead, there were several cases where whites took over schools that had previously been attended by blacks only. Schools such as West Virginia State College, Maryland State College, Bowie State College, and Delaware State College were state colleges attended by mostly black students. The majority of the student body of these and many other so-called black schools became white and began receiving adequate and equal money from the government.

While blacks were protesting, many whites were deciding how they would or could get around integration. They did not intend for their children to become inferior by attending inferior black schools. They did not want their tax money to be used to improve the quality of education being given out in black schools. They also did not want "inferior" black students attending white schools. Busing was out of the question, though black children had been bused past white schools to inferior black schools for years.

After the initial shock of all the talk of integration, some liberal whites joined the fun and protested also. That was just the way some viewed it, as apparently many blacks did. With so many different people protesting so many different things, the initial purpose of the protest marches was lost and blacks were back to square one again.

Whites took the slogan "black power" and changed it to "green power," "gray power," and even "white power." They adopted the hair styles (Afros and naturals), and Bo Derek (a white actress) popularized plaited braids. The black movement was so diluted and exploited that even blacks thought it was a fad or a phase that America was going through and that soon things would be back to normal.

Chapter 29
Separate but Equal

The philosophy of "separate but equal" was a poor one for the black and white races in America. The thing that was wrong with the implementation of this philosophy was it was left to the white race. With the white race totally in charge and dishonestly implementing programs, "separate but equal" failed as a solution to the black school problem in America.

Integration of the schools in America would have been a good idea if all things had been equal from the beginning and there had been some mutual respect. When blacks and whites viewed white as being the standard, this left the blacks trying to integrate with the whites. This made things one-sided from the beginning. Total integration is virtually impossible, especially when the standards reflect the state of one race's mind. Blacks who really feel that their children will receive a better education only because they are in a classroom with white students and white teachers cannot benefit from integration. Whites who feel that blacks are inferior and who do not wish for their children to be in the same classroom as black students or to be taught by black teachers cannot benefit from integration.

Integration in American schools has meant the further loss of black culture, heritage, and identity. Integration cannot and has not worked in America, because preferential treatment has been given to the white race where there have been attempts to integrate. Whites who are in charge of the department of education have a monumental problem in trying to integrate schools because of the numerous other racial problems in America. Taking care of the problem of child care, food, clothing, jobs, and many others that haunt the black race must take precedence over the problem of equal education and integration.

Integrating American schools, like everything else in America, will never be achieved unless a genuine effort is made first by the president of the United States and by the white people. Black people have done their darnedest to make integration work. Black people must decide what is quality education for black people and work toward achieving it. Integrating with whites just for the sake of integrating will not further the cause of blacks educationally in America.

Chapter 30
More on Integration

Integrating the schools without busing is impossible, because in many communities the majority of blacks live in the same area. Unfair housing laws and economic situations cause this to be true. It also seems perfectly natural that whites would want to live together in the same area, for whatever reasons, in as much as many people of certain races seem to do better together. Black Americans arc some of the few people who seek to live away from their own people even though there is a certain sense of security derived from living together among your own folks.

Seeking quality education is one thing. Seeking decent housing also makes good sense. But seeking to be with white students and in white schools in order to obtain quality education is ludicrous. It is also ridiculous to feel that only housing in white areas is decent housing, yet this seems to be the mentality of white and black Americans. Blacks enter so-called white schools, and some white parents withdraw their children. Blacks move into so-called white neighborhoods, and whites move.

Real estate brokers made a fortune in what was called block busting. They would sell a house located in an all-white neighborhood to a black for twice as much as the whites paid for it. The blacks would pay willingly—not for the better housing, but for the house that came with white neighbors. Then the real estate broker would go to the whites next door and tell them their neighborhood was turning black. This way he could sell their house to another black for more and in turn sell the white people a house in the suburbs. This would go on throughout white neighborhoods until the entire area was occupied by blacks. Then, contrary to the thinking of most people, the municipal services to the area would decrease. The trash was not picked up as often, and the streets weren't repaired and kept as clean as they had been when whites had lived in the area. Blacks would be blamed for the area's deterioration, and of course no one wanted this to happen to his or her neighborhood. It is not unexpected that whites spread such false information, but it is sad when blacks rate themselves poorly. Granted, some of their feelings of inferiority are based on fact, inasmuch as blacks have had fewer opportunities. Naturally, they knew less about taking care of things. Many blacks must work long hours, so their children might be in the streets destroying others' property. Blacks know these things and should find ways to circumvent them rather than run from them and talk about them.

"Birds of a feather flock together." White people have a right to want to live with people with whom they feel comfortable, but should know that as long as they keep decent things away from black Americans, they will be plagued with blacks trying to get to where they are or get what they have. It seems equal opportunity would eventually solve the problems.

Chapter 31
Racism on the Job

Civil service jobs, though controlled by the government, are just like all other jobs. They are managed by white people, and most of the workers in the government are white Many times blacks are the last to be hired for any given civil service job and the first to be fired. If the job is prestigious or involves large sums of money, often whites are hired. If the job is low-paying, dirty, and/or temporary, often blacks are hired. Black workers who have to remain on the job longer because fewer jobs and fewer promotions are available to them usually inherit a supervisory position, in contrast with the white worker who is usually ap pointed to such positions. Whites, who often gain their experience through blacks who have been on the job for long periods of time, are usually moved to higher positions and often supervise the black people who trained them.

Few blacks are appointed to high-paying jobs in the government except where there is a need for a black face for so-called window dressing. In that case, he or she is a face, not a voice, and is not expected to perform a real job.

Many blacks in the government obtained their jobs through friends. Seldom if ever are blacks called from the civil service register. Like everything else, it's who you know, not what you know. Because blacks are not in the important hiring and firing positions, they get to bring in few other blacks. When a supervisor or other person in a position to hire someone wishes to hire a black, he simply goes to one of his black workers for a recommendation. Many white personnel officers still reserve the right to decide if the recommendation is suitable or not.

A black person's character is always highly scrutinized before he is hired on a civil service job. His record usually is expected to be impeccable, and a recommendation from the local minister is often given the greatest consideration.

As it was immediately after slavery, it is hard for many young black men to grow up without having been arrested. This means many black men are excluded from civil service jobs, which usually require the applicant to have a clean record. With even small infractions of the law keeping black men out of the work force, this situation virtually compels them to become in volved in more crime in order to survive. Many white people live in environments that are considered wholesome and crime free and are protected by the law rather than arrested; therefore, their records are not apt to be marred with minor arrests. When a black boy is picked up by the police, more often than not he is arrested. When a white boy is picked up by the police, more often than not he is released or deposited with his parents at home.

I got my government job after college through my cousin, who had been working at the Department of Agriculture for more than twenty years. The Department of Agriculture was known throughout the black community for being the most racist department of all and the last to hire black s. The fact that my cousin had been there as long as he had and was still only a GS-3 should have been enough to inform me of the kind of department it was. (GS stood for Grade Status. Government jobs go from GS-I to GS-18.) I had come to Washington, D.C., seeking employment, and like most of the blacks there, I was anxious to get a job in the government. For the most part, the kind of job, the grade, and the salary were totally irrelevant. Like many blacks seeking employment, I was willing to do any kind of work.

Many of the blacks working in the government were low-paid secretaries, messengers, or janitors. Almost all of the men went to work in their best clothes and changed at their lockers after arriving at work. I was hired because my cousin had recommended me to his supervisor. Without asking my qualifications, this man took me to the personnel officer and signed me up for the job. I was hired as a handyman at the bottom of the pay scale. A week or two later, I filled out an application. I was working in the sub-basement of the agriculture building and wore a suit, shirt, and tie to work just like the other black men, though my job consisted of moving desks and file cabinets. Most of the workers that I delivered desks or cabinets to in the department had less education than I had. I was working with three other blacks, two GS-1s who were illiterate and one GS-3, a seventy-three-year-old supervisor. There were at least two or three blacks in the building (a twelve-story building) who were GS-5s and who spent no time with blacks who worked at lesser grades.

Though the United States government was supposed to have been an Equal Opportunity Employer, there were twice as many whites in the government as there were blacks. Though there were many blacks living in the District of Columbia, the number of blacks working in the government did not reflect the population of the city. Though there were many other government jobs in other cities in America, there were very few blacks working on government jobs outside of Washington, D.C. (as post office janitors, farm equipment demonstrators, and so on).

Why did I take a job as a handyman when I had a college education (a bachelor of science degree in health education)? Because I had spent months walking along blocks, going from government building to government building, trying to obtain employment. I was told at each personnel office that I was overqualified or underqualified. I felt that qualifications were a factor only when it came to hiring black people. Blacks are almost always more qualified than whites. White workers were allowed to acquire experience on the job. Blacks are expected to have experience and training in order to be hired on most jobs. I was turned down because I lacked experience at jobs that required a degree and those that did not require a degree. I wondered how you could get experience if no one would hire you. A friend of mine who was also seeking employment but did not have a degree obtained a job weeks before I did. My degree pigeonholed me and faked me into thinking I would be able to do more or better in a position that required a degree. The color of my skin seemed to have been my biggest problem. Apparently, the white people in charge of hiring had preconceived notions as to what a person for certain position should look like. They didn't picture blacks in positions other than as messengers, janitors, and secretaries. Though there was not supposed to be discrimination in hiring, the rules might have changed, but the game was still the same. I took a job as a GS-I with a college degree because I couldn't get any other job. Like other blacks, I was forced to take a job to survive, and I was obliged to remain on this job longer than I intended to, because I didn't earn enough money from payday to payday to take time off and look for another job. I also knew there were few, if any, other jobs available for blacks. A government job was what blacks sought, because these jobs were supposed to guarantee security and status. I learned a government job was the same as any other job for a black, except you could go to work dressed up. For the kind of jobs most blacks were performing, overalls were more suitable, and that's what they should have been wearing to work.

    I remained on the job at the Department of Agriculture for about six months, at which time I was recommended by a friend for a job with the Department of Public Welfare. I was hired by this agency for a position with the title institutional counselor, and my grade level was GS-3. My salary moved up to $3,175. Here again my college degree had nothing to do with the job I was performing at the children's center, because the center's work consisted mostly of warehousing black indigent children.

The children's center had just opened recently, in 1954, and had been forced to integrate because of the 1954 school decision (Brown versus Ferguson). This proved to be a problem, because the population of the District of Columbia was rapidly changing from mostly white to mostly black.

The original plans were to take the white delinquent boys from the Industrial Home School (IHS) on lily-white Wisconsin Avenue and put them at Maple Glen. (This was an established school for white delinquent boys from the District of Columbia located in Laurel, Maryland.) The delinquent black boys and girls at Blue Plains School (a school for black delinquents) located in the blighted southeastern area of the District were slated to go to Cedar Knoll. This school was being constructed and was also located in Laurel, Maryland. Cedar Knoll School was purposefully located away from the other District training schools located in Laurel, Maryland, because it was being constructed strictly for black delinquents. The 1954 decision to integrate schools caught the establishment with no plans to pave the road leading to Cedar Knoll. Construction of the school improved tremendously, how ever, when they realized white delinquents would have to be committed there along with the black delinquents. The road was paved in time for the dedication ceremony.

Cedar Knoll continued to be considered the District's school for black delinquents because of the number of black children that were transferred there from Blue Plains School. For this reason, the Department of Welfare authorities were reluctant to move the white boys from IHS to Cedar Knoll. They released as many of them as they could into the community. They transferred the majority of the white boys that they couldn't release to Maple Glen, which they had decided to continue to use for delinquent boys from the District (black or white).

The few so-called aggressive white boys were placed at Cedar Knoll with the greatest of care and protection. (I haven't the slightest idea where they kept the delinquent white girls from the District.)

The white boys at Cedar Knoll were protected in that the white administrators from IHS were placed in the top administrative jobs at Cedar Knoll when the transfers were made. The black administrators from Blue Plains School were made their assistants. All of the black assistant administrators' education and experience levels were higher than those of the white administrators. Most of the white administrators were retired workers (do-gooders) who wanted to work with indigent or poor people for self-gratification. The jobs at Cedar Knoll were considered good jobs for the black workers, who were happy to be working. Most whites who worked there used the job to gain experience or to become experts and consultants on the subject of juvenile delinquents. At Cedar Knoll, they spent a considerable amount of their time protecting the white delinquent boys, who were in the minority there.

I was the youngest counselor at Cedar Knoll and enjoyed working with the young black boys, whom I didn't consider to be delinquents, as the other black workers did. I was happy to have a job in the government with such an important-sounding title. The grade and salary were not important, and I had no idea what a real juvenile delinquent was supposed to be like. I was well aware, however, that the white administrators at Cedar Knoll were insensitive to the needs of the blacks there, who were more dependent than delinquent.

The first incident of racism I witnessed there was when a very competent white secretary was fired after it was established that she had shown too much interest in one of the black counselors at the school. This was not the reason given for dismissing the secretary, but everybody was well aware of the real reason it had happened.

None of the white boys was considered aggressive, therefore, none of them was placed in any of the cottages designated for aggressive boys. The white boys, who had been carefully placed in the so-called cottages for mildly delinquent boys, were still complaining of being harassed and attacked by the black boys. This information was passed on to the general superintendent of the children's center and later to the superintendent of the Department of Public Welfare. These were the two top people in the administration, with tremendous other duties. It seems their sub ordinates could have covered what happened to be such a small matter. On the contrary, the superintendent himself went to Cedar Knoll (which was eighteen miles from his office) that very evening and told the chief counselor to transfer all of the white boys to one side of each cottage, so they could protect each other. He stated that if this order was not carried out that night, "heads would roll." He further informed the chief counselor that one of the heads might be his.

The chief counselor and the assistant superintendent were both very competent black men. They found it very difficult to work under such biased conditions. Both turned to the bottle, and the highly admired assistant administrator died of heart failure at a very young age. Both these men had been demoted and locked into non-policy-making positions simply because of the color of their skin. This is a hard pill to swallow, not to mention what it does to one's initiative. As Browning wrote, "A man's reach should exceed his grasp, or what's a heaven for?"

After a while, I could no longer ignore the fact that more time and care were lavished upon white students than with black students. When I brought this and other problems to the attention of the administration, I was admonished severely and virtually told to mind my own business. When I pursued the matter further during a joint staff meeting, I was told by the general administrator that Cedar Knoll was considered to be a black institution because 87 percent of the student body was black.

It was interesting how the administrators organized a network to protect the few white students at Cedar Knoll. I wondered if such network would have been considered if the black children had been in the minority.

It was obvious I wouldn't be going far as a counselor at Cedar Knoll. The general superintendent shook my hand and commended me for vigorously pursuing answers to what I thought was a problem. I had been around white people enough to know that the same network that had been formed to protect white children was used daily to keep blacks like me in place.

The white students were continuously released from the children's center until the last one was gone. The District's population was by this time almost totally black, so very few white students were being committed to Cedar Knoll.

Since I had been persistent about discussing racial matters, I was locked into the job as a counselor, with no real hopes of ever becoming a senior counselor. Remaining at the same grade level for a long length of time appeared to indicate a worker was incompetent. Some of my co-workers told me to smile more and I would certainly be promoted. I was considered an excellent worker among my fellow workers. Unfortunately, they were not the ones who gave the recommendations when I applied for other jobs. The same people I had been persistent with concerning racial problems were responsible for my recommendations. As other job administrators were white, it was easy enough for one of my white sponsors to give me a good recommendation on paper and condemn me later with a phone call, or over a cocktail or a cup of coffee. Most of the administrators for the District government were white, lived in the same neighborhoods in and around the city, and stayed in frequent contact with each other. After I had worked for thirteen years at the children's center, a friend of mine called me from the D.C. juvenile court and suggested that I apply for the job as probation officer that was vacant there. Again, my papers were walked through and I was hired without reservations. This was the only way I could have gotten away from the children's center, though my records indicate I was an excellent worker.

The job at juvenile court appeared to be a "piece of cake" for blacks who were employed there. Though nine-tenths of the cases that the court dealt with concerned blacks, the chief judge and one of the other two judges were white. The hearing officers and the court clerk were white. Eight of the ten supervisors and the chief probation officers supervisor were white. Though blacks who worked there acted like they had important positions, most of them were messengers, secretaries, or probation officers with impossible case loads. Racism was well camouflaged, but blacks had but to open their eyes to see it was still there.

Johnny Van Dossen (not his real name) was the only white boy on my case load. He, his brother, and his mother were the only white people living in the all-black Clifton Terrace apartments in the heart of inner-city Washington. Johnny, with his red hair and freckles, was a modern-day Huck Finn and the darling of all his black neighbors. He had an innocent smile that was disarming, but he was just as delinquent as any other twelve-year old on my case load.

Johnny's mother brought him to my office one afternoon. Her face was tearful when she told me he was beyond her control and requested that I lock him up. She said she could no longer be responsible for his delinquent behavior. I told her that she could sign the proper papers and I would hold Johnny in the receiving home until he could be seen by a judge. Johnny was calm and acted as though he did not mind being removed from his home. Most of the delinquents being held at the receiving home were faring better there than they had been at home, as far as food and personal needs were concerned.

Johnny was brought before a judge for a preliminary hearing, at which time he was remanded to the receiving home until such time as his case could be investigated by his probation officer.

That Friday afternoon I was reminded once again of how white people take care of each other, when I received a call from Johnny's court-appointed lawyer. He said, "Mr. Faison, I'm taking Johnny out of that receiving home and taking him home with me. That place is no place for a little boy like Johnny," he said. I said okay because I knew he and no one else was authorized to take Johnny from the receiving home without my signature. I had not planned to sign Johnny out of the receiving home for the reason the lawyer had given me, because suitable or not, that was the facility the District had designated to hold their delinquents until they went to court. Johnny was no different from any of the other twelve-year-olds being held there.

My plans changed within the next five minutes, because the chief judge called me and said, "Mr. Faison, I want you to go over to the receiving home and sign Johnny Van Dossen out to Attorney Palson for the weekend." I had seen white-collar people have their cases adjudicated in the judge's chambers, but this was a brand new experience for me. I had wondered why fewer and fewer white children had been committed to the children's center before I left. The blacker Cedar Knoll's population became, the fewer white boys and girls were committed there. They were being protected from an all-black situation even at the level of the courts.

Attorney Palson was in my office when I arrived at work Monday morning. Johnny had run away from the plush setting the lawyer had provided for him for the weekend and returned to Clifton Terrace. He stole the lawyer's son's bicycle for transportation home.

The lawyer displayed a very arrogant attitude in my office, because he knew I had felt Johnny would do exactly what he had done. He was still very adamant about Johnny's not returning to the receiving home, however, but felt some other limits should be set for Johnny. He and the chief judge drew up some rules for Johnny to follow, such as: being in the house before dark, attending school regularly, staying out of trouble in the community, et cetera. This was a joke to Johnny, and he knew he had us all squirming.

The racism had just begun. The continuation date of Johnny's hearing in court was due, and I was well prepared. I had planned first to tell Judge Fectin, who had committed Johnny to the receiving home originally, how the chief judge had dealt with his case underhandedly. I had presumed they had not collaborated with each other about the case, since Johnny had been committed. I discovered on the day of the hearing that I was wrong. First of all, the bailiff did not announce the time the case was being heard in court until it had already begun. The judge, Attorney Palson, Johnny. and his mother were all in the courtroom. When I entered the courtroom, they all turned and looked at me, and together they looked very obviously white. They continued to discuss Johnny's case as though what I had to say was not important. Attorney Palson told the Judge he had probably learned more about Johnny in the few weeks he had been working with the case than I had learned the entire time I had been assigned to the case. The judge turned to me abruptly and said, "Mr. Faison, what have you done with Johnny's case since the preliminary hearing?" I began by explaining to the judge that Johnny's mother had brought him to my office and requested that I remove him from her home because he was beyond her control. At that moment, Johnny's mother burst out in tears and said, "That's not true. I want my Johnny home with me." It was apparent that this was a no-win situation. Here was a case of a black man trying to get a white boy committed to a black institution over the heads of three white people. Johnny was obviously winning, with the judge, his lawyer, and his mother on his side.

The judge asked me what my plans were for Johnny, and I recommended he be committed to Maple Glen School. The judge looked at me scornfully and snarled, "What good will that do, Mr. Faison? "Before I could answer him, he said, "You can't tell me this young man is a threat to the community." I noticed my voice was quivering when I told the judge that Maple Glen was where the court had been sending young delinquents who were beyond the control of their parent or parents. He closed Johnny's folder and said, "Mr. Faison, I'm continuing this case for two weeks to give you time to come up with a viable program for Johnny. If you don't have an acceptable plan for him when we return in two weeks, I will find you in contempt of this court." He slammed the mallet down and said, "Case continued for two weeks."

I could hardly believe what had just happened to me. I felt as though I had been sentenced to two weeks of hard labor, because of something I had done to Johnny. As I was leaving the courtroom, I noticed Johnny and his mother and lawyer and the judge were standing around the judge's bench as though they were discussing the aspects of the case I wasn't suppose to hear. It appeared to be a white-only conversation, and I was well aware that justice was not color-blind.

Upon returning to my office, I discovered the word had already gotten to my supervisor, Mr. Hegendorf. He came to my office shortly afterward and suggested that I explore the possibility of placing Johnny in the Hershey School for Boys, in Hershey, Pennsylvania (the home of the Hershey candy bar and the Hershey Amusement Park). When he gave me the pamphlet he had in his hand describing the school, I noticed the picture of three white boys on the cover. I asked Mr. Hegendorf if the school was for white boys, and he hedged by saying, "I don't know Faison; I never really looked into that aspect of the school." When I researched the possibility of Johnny becoming enrolled in the school, I learned it not only was segregated, but it was supposedly stipulated by the founder

(Mr. Hershey) that the school was to remain segregated as long as it stood.

There were few blacks living in Hershey, a few black janitors working at the Hershey candy factory, and no blacks working at the Hershey Amusement Park. This was what Hershey, Pennsylvania was about, in a nutshell.

The fact that this was in the year of 1967 and the decision had been passed in 1954 had no bearing in this case because the Hershey School for Boys was a private school. The D.C. juvenile court (D.C. citizens) paid for Johnny to attend this segregated school.

No other student from my case load was ever sent to the Hershey School for Boys, especially inasmuch ac; from then on my case load consisted of black boys only.

0 0 0

The following is an essay written by one of my former co-workers, Ralph Reynard. He presented it to me at my retirement party, where I was given a standing ovation by the 450 people who attended. I feel this paper is a tribute to the way I was on my job and how many co-workers felt about me.

After having been given the African title Owusu, I gave a lot of thought to giving up my slave name Faison. I felt Owusu was very appropriate in that I was "a clearer of the ways" for most of my co-workers.

At that time, I didn't know if I should try to be more African or try to be more American. Like many blacks in America, I was very confused, attempting to achieve in a country where all of the odds were against me. I felt it was time to decide who I was going to be in America. This is a decision blacks in America have to make in order to begin to make progress as a race.

After a great deal of thought over a long period of time, I decided I am an American.

In spite of the fact that I would like to be totally African, I cannot escape the situation others blacks and I find ourselves in.

I decided to accept the fact that I can only be African-American and identify with the mother continent Africa in as many ways and as often as possible.

The fact that I am American means I must also learn to live in America in spite of the racism and the obstacles we African Americans encounter because of the color of our skin.

I shall forever cherish the African title Owusu that was be stowed upon me by Ralph.

Liberation—A Tribute to Owusu Eddie Faison*

Liberation raised his head high and proclaimed—once again, yet another time—I will descend unto the earth.

But this time his instrument was not as one free but one bound yet destined to go from "slaveship to championship."

From the big fast country of North Carolina to the Capitol Dome in D.C., "Liberation" through this one would lead, liberate, and *educate*, for he is *Owusu, Clearer of the Way*. His way is that of Malcolm.

"By any means necessary." And he stands as did Malcolm—*a symbol of our black manhood.*

Liberation began his landmark through this one called Owusu, Eddie Faison. P.E. classes were informally held daily before the workday began. P.E. in this instance does not mean physical education but political education. In those days one did not need Maxwell House, Lipton's, *"Doonesberry,"* the cross word, *Jigsaw*, or the Metro section for eye openers. Because the daily drum of Owusu Eddie Faison was the sounding board and forum where a free exchange and interchange of ideas and ideals were deliberated and debated.

He created an atmosphere of treating others as human beings and with respect *as a man or as a woman* when working with clients, co-workers and in *dealing with* management *literally* and *figuratively*, as when it was necessary to ask management

-YOU WILL KICK WHOSE A--?

This reminds one of the strategic geographical boundaries on the Corrections obstacle course. Many were the landmarks throughout the years, inclusive of but by no means limited to the following: (Please acknowledge as the roll is called. Any re semblance in name is purely coincidental.)

Martin's Domain
Schuman's Lookout Mountain
Porter's peninsula
Dennison's Junction Swain on the Plain
Wade cross the Water at Brown's PointManson's Lagoon
Zimmerman's Bend
Taylor's Swamp at Point Crossroads
Woods across the Road
Kibler's Island
Stone's Bayou
Harry's Hollow

The FYCA Commandos, later better known as Wilson's Mavericks, from the 13th Street Outpost have provided the lite support system, as Brother Owusu Eddie Faison has run and finished this Correction's Obstacle Course.

Owusu Eddie Faison
"From Slaveship to Championship"*

Owusu Eddie Faison
"From Slaveship to Championship"

He would say, in so many words: -Throw off the redneck **KKK** slave mentality-Avoid a hypocritical black bourgeoise attitude-Stand fast among the people for

"WE ARE THE PEOPLE"

He is a master gamesman who treats life as the greatest of all games.

O WU SU EDD IE   FAISON.

He is not so much a man ahead of his time as *a man in his time. Standing up, speaking out and taking a stand when one's manhood demands such action necessary.*

A people's champ, which meant leading many unpopular causes, which also meant being challenged by a topheavy and insensitive bureaucracy because he was perceived as being a threat to *racism, oppression and exploitation-and* rightly so.

"But no matter how it is shaken, the cream always rises to the top."

So to our beloved friend andbrother
Owusu Eddie Faison.
"From Slaveship to Championship"
Owusu Eddie Faison
"From Slaveship to Championship"

He passed onto us a mentality and tradition of survival techniques which has sustained our people throughout the generations and which will ultimately restore our people to their traditional greatness, because we have come together in unity for life's sake and chosen to name ourselves, define ourselves, speak/or ourselves and not to be named, defined and spoken for by those alien to black survival and the people's struggle. He has led and liberated us in these struggles which do now at this very hour continue and will continue, for liberation from exploitation-which this man symbolizes-is an external vigil.

"From Slaveship to Championship" *he symbolizes our black manhood as emancipated from physical and mental slavery.*
Owusu Eddie Faison-Clearer of the Way.
And Liberation looked down and again beheld his landmark as wrought through this appointed one, and he proclaimed unto the generations:

"From Slaveship to Championship"
Owusu Eddie Faison
"From Slaveship to Championship"
Owusu Eddie Faison.
"From Slaveship to Championship"
Owusu Eddie Faison

Kahlil Opia Lasana
(Ralph Reynuad)
Friend, Liberated Poet

Chapter 32
Malcolm X—a Great Antiracist of His Day

I remember Rosa Parks, who one day decided she didn't want to go to the back of the bus in Alabama. This was the incident that brought Martin Luther King, Jr., to the forefront. It also was probably the single event that caused blacks to begin to see them selves as human beings rather than ex-slaves. If they had made this realization and come together as a race, earlier blacks would have probably been well on the way to being respected human beings in America, instead of second-class citizens. Shortsighted ness on the part of black leaders caused them to expend their energies attempting to integrate and become more like the white people who had enslaved them.

Malcolm X was born Malcolm Little, in Omaha, Nebraska. He was an intelligent child, but was told by one of his white instructors he should seek blue-collar work because of his lack of ability.

Malcolm saw his father taken away from their home one night by white men, and Malcolm never saw his father again. His mother later became mentally unstable and soon died in a home for the mentally ill.

Malcolm then moved to Massachusetts, where he lived with his sister and worked as a janitor in a theater. This is where he began to learn to be "city slick." He moved to New York after a few years and became known as Detroit Red, the king of the streets of Harlem. He hung out in the famous nightclubs in Harlem and dealt in dope, women, and everything else that was profitable.

Malcolm was arrested in 1946, found guilty of a crime, and sentenced to ten years in prison. He used this time in prison to find himself. He educated himself by studying the dictionary and every other book available to him in and out of the prison. He felt that since he had nothing but time, he should use that time wisely.

While in prison, Malcolm adopted the Islamic religion and became a messenger for The Honorable Elijah Muhammad. Malcolm dropped his last name, which he said had come from the white slave master, and replaced it with an X. He began preaching to black people about helping themselves.

Malcolm X was paroled to the community in 1952 a changed man. He had the nerve to return to the streets of Harlem, where he had hustled for a living, and preach to the same men he had associated with before going to jail. He urged his former partners in crime to give up their slave names and help pull the black race together. He was the one who said a big black nose did not have to be ugly, just because it didn't look like the white man's narrow nose. Malcolm X said our big lips did not have to be unsightly because they were not thin like the white man's lips. He was smart enough to know kinky hair was not bad hair, just because white folks' straight hair was the standard used in America for good hair.

Malcolm X preached self-help to black people, because it was obvious no one else was going to help us. It seems white people would have approved of Malcolm's teaching and preaching self-help to black people inasmuch as over the years they had said that black people should help themselves.

Malcolm X had foresight enough to know as long as black people remained black, they would never be accepted as equal to the white race. Therefore he spent most of his adult life attempting to get blacks to wake up and help themselves. Malcolm thought being equal to the white man should not be the most important goal for a black person. He also thought it should not be important to a black man or a white man whether a black man loved a white man or not.

I saw Malcolm X on television for the first time in the late 1950s, explaining himself to James Farmer, Wyatt T. Walker, and a white interviewer. Malcolm seemed to have had so much nerve that I got goose pimples as I listened to him and watched him speak. I had never seen a black man hold his head up and speak negatively about white people as Malcolm did. I had only seen black people speak to and of white people apologetically.

James Farmer said on television that day blacks were making tremendous progress with race relations and civil rights in the South. He reminded the panel that in Greensboro, North Carolina, blacks were going to the theaters with white people and sitting beside them in restaurants. Malcolm X smiled as he told Mr. Farmer that after four hundred years that could hardly be considered progress. He asked him why he wanted to attend a movie or sit beside a person who did not want him to sit beside him. It was very apparent that Malcolm X had done his homework and was ahead of the other panelists on the subject of race relations. He also was in a totally different world from the other two blacks on the panel, which was a rude awakening for Americans, black and white.

Malcolm X let it be known on television that evening that he was a Muslim and a prophet of the Honorable Elijah Muhammad. The following day, the media were saturated with headlines reading "Black Muslim Hates White People," though Malcolm at no time during the interview referred to the Muslims as Black Muslims. The media were anxious to get to Malcolm X again. and he was invited back to that television program the following Sunday. Malcolm X was smart enough not to return, however, knowing the deck would have been stacked against him. He had caught white and black America by surprise. White men had never had a black man look them in the face and say, "I don't like you," even after the peculiar institution of slavery had been abolished. Blacks had thought they were speaking for all blacks when they expressed their desire to integrate with white people.

Malcolm X was saying to blacks to get it for themselves and no one could take it away from them. He knew when someone gives you something, they can also take it away. He knew human rights were what blacks were seeking in America, though human rights are supposedly God-given rights. Malcolm X was aware that the Constitution gave all American people civil rights and if blacks were considered Americans, there should have been no need for a civil rights bill for black people. He knew so very well that he was often misunderstood by whites and, unfortunately, by blacks also. He was thought by both races to be a threat to the progress blacks were supposedly making in race relations and civil rights.

Malcolm X visited Mecca and learned that Muslims were of many colors and races of people. He learned they were all human beings. He later broke away from the Muslims and Elijah Muhammad and formed his own organization. His organization was known as Black Nationalists because Malcolm was well aware that a people without a nation to identify with are powerless.

I watched Malcolm X preaching on the streets of Harlem and on television and feared for his life. I knew racist America would not allow him to continue to live and preach unity to black people. Throughout the history of blacks in America, whites have fought blacks coming together for any reason except for religion, because of the threat they would present to whites as a unit. They have always kept blacks divided by one method or another, because they know as long as blacks are divided, they will not be a problem for the white race. "A house divided against itself cannot stand."

Malcolm X continued to spread the word in the United States and abroad until he was killed in New York on February 21, 1965. Though blacks killed him, I felt that they were merely tools for the white men who made blacks think Malcolm X was black people's enemy rather than their friend. I believe the white power structure could not afford to let Malcolm X live, so they strategically killed him through his own people.

Upon Malcolm X's death, some blacks began to realize the message he was trying to get across to them. Most blacks had previously dismissed his ideology as idle talk or words from a "crazy black man." They had no idea of the intelligence of this man. He was obviously born ahead of his time and was killed before blacks realized the impact he could have had on the race in general. He was truly a revolutionary, and I was not surprised when he was killed. White racist America has never tolerated black men whom they could not control.

Chapter 33
The March on Washington

I was at the march on Washington in August 1963. I had made the District of Columbia my home after graduating from school and was gainfully employed.

I don't know why it was called the march on Washington instead of the march in Washington, because Washington controlled the march. It was an enjoyable outing for all involved. Black and white together, arm in arm, old and young, rich and poor-all marched to the Lincoln Memorial. Again I felt like we all were people with love for each other. It was a wonderful feeling. We enjoyed the speech by Martin Luther King, Jr., about a dream he had about black kids and white kids living harmoniously together. It was obviously more of a nightmare that he had, and of course as long as he thought he was dreaming, white America had no problem with it. Though 213,000 people marched that day, the white establishment, especially in D.C., was not bothered because they told them how come, when to come, where to go, and how long to stay. The Washington Post, which had mapped everything out for the marchers, acclaimed the march a success the following morning. They said the last marcher was safely out of the city by 8:30 P.M. and the city was back to normal. Fun was had by all, and the brief visit that the Reverend King and the other so-called black spokesmen had with the president, asking for blacks' civil rights, was history. I have yet to figure out why blacks need civil rights bills passed in order to obtain civil rights in America. I am well aware that the Bill of Rights was not written for blacks, but I don't know why it can't apply to us now that we are supposed to be free and Americans.

By that Monday morning, I was back to normal, again realizing I was black in a white racist world.

Martin Luther King, Jr., truly believed he could make a difference, so he continued to march and protest. When he moved out of the impossible area of integration into the area of the Vietnam War, white America became concerned. He had over stepped his boundaries, and shortly afterward he was killed.

Chapter 34
The 1968 Riots in D.C.

Ironically enough, Martin Luther King's death sparked riots all over the United States. I was in Northwest Washington when the

D.C. riot began. Stokely Carmichael (Kwanme Turare), who had been a student in the District at Howard University, stood on the hood of a car at Fourteenth and U Street Northwest and begged the crowd of mostly black males not to riot. He told them that was not the way. It was later inferred that he incited the crowd to riot, but that was not true. The crowd was angry and unruly because their leader, Martin Luther King, Jr., had been killed. The time was right, because blacks were feeling that white America was only pacifying them with crumbs here and there and giving them lip service about concern for blacks' problems.

Northwest Washington resembled one big forest fire by 11:00 A.M. the following day. I was a probation officer at D.C. juvenile court, where a memorandum was circulated instructing workers to go home. Ninety-nine percent of the white government workers lived outside of the city, in Virginia or Maryland. Black D.C. residents knew this, so some of them stationed themselves at the Maryland and Virginia lines, where whites had to pass in order to get out of the city, and pummeled their cars with rocks and bottles. Word got around that cars that had "soul brother" written on them would be spared. Blacks and whites who lived outside the District desperately looked for something with which to write "soul brother" on their cars.

White people also owned almost all of the stores and businesses in the District. They closed their doors, wrote "soul brother" on their showcase windows and cars, and fled the city.

When the blacks were left in the city, rioting, burning, and looting, former white District residents realized the mistake they had made by moving to the suburbs in the first place and leaving the capital to the black District residents.

The D.C. policemen were baffled. This was the first time they had been faced with the question of whether to kill a person over property or not. Women, men, and children were looting stores in broad daylight as the doors were broken down. Some had wheelbarrows and made several trips. Some even rented trucks and backed them up to the doors of the stores and loaded up. After the stores were looted, most of them were set on fire. The police for the most part stood by while this was taking place. They were waiting for instructions from the mayor or one of his subordinates on how to handle this new and very different kind of problem.

A curfew was placed on the city, and troops came in from Fort Bragg, Fort Meade, and Quantico Marine Base. I watched them set up pup tents on the football field of Woodson Junior High School down the street from my house. The weapons, trucks, and helicopters were frightening, not to mention the soldiers, who were apparently dressed and prepared for war.

Army guards were placed at every entrance and exit of the District and on every major street in the inner city. Anyone caught on the streets after curfew without proper identification was arrested. Washington, D.C. was an armed camp.

The looting stopped and the rioting and burning subsided. A new black emerged from the experience, however, and the capital has not been the same since.

Blacks who made public statements on television and radio and said blacks had only hurt themselves by rioting and burning were realizing that their statements had been made prematurely. Blacks did not own enough to hurt themselves.

Those who lived on top of white-owned rat- and roach-infested stores had little or nothing to lose.

Liquor stores, mom-and-pop grocery stores, and small clothing stores were the hardest hit, so the owners of these stores were the biggest losers.

There was a liquor store on every comer, and on some of the busy comers there were two liquor stores. Stores this close to a residential neighborhood were tempting to all alcoholics and potential alcoholics.

The mom-and-pop grocery stores were also white-owned. There were little old white men and women selling inferior grocery products in every black community. They sold these products at much higher prices than the major supermarkets. They sold junk food and soda to every kid that had a nickel or dime and preyed upon those who could not or would not make it to the major supermarkets. They kept poor people on the hook by allowing them to keep a tab (buy on credit). They kept the books and padded them any way they wanted.

The white-owned clothing stores were the same as the mom and-pop grocery stores. They sold inferior merchandise for exorbitant prices. They also allowed people to buy on time. Some of the stores had been in the same neighborhood for many years and have kept families on tab from one generation to other.

These merchants would close their stores in the evening, get in their big cars, and go home to Maryland and Virginia. They paid taxes where they lived. They took from the inner city where blacks were forced to remain and gave nothing in return.

During the summer, there were few jobs created for the young black people in the District. The merchants would hire their own children or some other white youngsters for the summer. The black community became fed up to the point of explosion.

Whites who had previously owned everything reluctantly returned to the District. They too had gone through a transformation. Their attitudes toward the District residents were somewhat different, and as they rebuilt their businesses they definitely had blacks in mind. Most of them hired blacks or at least one black to indicate to this new black city that they were concerned. Some hired blacks for their own protection. Many of them got tough and armed themselves, only to become nervous wrecks. Most of them were not accustomed to being armed and found it difficult to deal with a weapon on a daily basis. Iron bars were constructed at the doors and the windows of most stores, and whites stopped parking their big cars with Maryland and Virginia license plates in front of their places of business. They treated their black customers like they were people, for a change.

Blacks walked in stores like they were purchasing goods, as they were, as opposed to begging. They became aware that they were spending their money and that the merchants were depending on them for a living.

When they began to rebuild the District, they did it with black people in mind. Whites who had previously felt free to come into the District and take were viewing black people from a different perspective. Some had the task of rebuilding their burned out places completely, while some had but to remodel. Others chose to board up their stores and abandon their businesses completely. Those who rebuilt and remodeled provided jobs for many black contractors. Those who chose not to return helped the community because they were no longer there to take from and exploit the people.

Blacks were hired to operate many of the businesses, because some whites were afraid or refused to return to the District. Some whites tried to deal with their new problems by bringing in stronglooking young white men who were very visible. Most of them gave in sooner or later and hired blacks in some capacity. They also began an attempt to provide quality products for their customers.

Blacks were learning skills in marketing for the first time in their lives. Management and ownership were changing from white to black at a rapid pace, because blacks were learning how easy it was to get something for nothing and sell it to those who were gullible.

I enjoyed living in the District during the seventies because of the black mentality that existed there. Blacks were the rule rather than the exception and proud of it. Having a mayor in our own image made it seem like he belonged to each individual citizen, somewhat like white people having a God in their own image. The same became true for the city council, school board, and most of the other political positions and department heads in the District. The children in the District, especially the black male children, grew up loving themselves, with strong black role models to emulate.

White people realized the mistake they made by leaving American cities to be managed by blacks. Several major cities (Detroit, Gary, and Newark) were abandoned by whites who sought a better living in the suburbs with white neighbors.

Blacks are enjoying their last stronghold in American cities. Whites are returning to the cities in large numbers for many reasons. The real estate brokers and the housing authorities are cooperating with them by allowing the prices for housing to be out of the reach of most blacks, who often need a house with at least three bedrooms. Soon American cities will be occupied by whites again and blacks will never have the opportunity to control the inner city again.

Chapter 35

How a Few Blacks Got Rich

Blacks have achieved more fame and fortune in America through sports and music than any other avenues. It was strictly coincidental that this happened, because they had performed these services for whites and blacks over the years for little or no pay.

Black people were great singers, dancers, and athletes before they were brought to America. After being enslaved in America, they continued to display their talents in many ways. The slave owners would often recognize special abilities and talents among their slaves and pit them against each other. They sometimes competed against slaves from other plantations. Matching one slave against another became very popular, and their owners saw where money could be made from such activities.

Slaves who had exceptional talents always received preferential treatment. They were entertainers for the white folks on weekends, holidays, and other special occasions. They got their practice and entertained each other daily in the cotton and tobacco fields. They got to wear the uniforms, costumes and different beautiful-colored outfits that were reserved for entertainers only. They were the master's favorites and even got to wear a big hat like the master's on occasions. Of course they were the envy of their fellow slaves.

Black people were religious and rhythmic. They sang and danced in the church and in the fields. They also whooped it up in the same fashion on Saturday after work and on Sundays after church. Many of them had exceptional voices and were chosen to entertain blacks and whites. They would compete against each other in the cotton fields and in church on Sunday. White men would take their talented slaves to perform for pay. The slave owners retained the pay, however, and the slaves received a pat on the back.

After slavery was abolished, talented African-Americans still entertained blacks and whites for little or no pay. Though they were considered to be celebrities among their peers, they were still blacks as far as the whites they entertained were concerned. Their sole purpose for being in a white establishment was to entertain. Dancers, musicians, and singers changed clothes and took their breaks in the kitchen with the cooks and other black help. The band members would have to take their breaks in front of or in back of the buildings. Entertainers who spent the night in a city had to stay with black friends or family, no matter how famous they were, because they were not allowed to stay in the white hotels and there were few, if any, black hotels. They were not allowed to mingle with the white guests and patrons they were entertaining under almost any circumstances. Even when this was allowed, it was not advisable and usually worked against them, because it would appear that they thought they were white. When a white felt a black had gotten so big that he or she was acting and thinking as if he or she were white, the white would cut the black down a notch or two. This meant they did not book the black in their clubs or attend the games or matches in which this particular person was involved (blackballing).

Jack Johnson, the first black heavyweight champion of the world, not only acted and dressed like he was white, but he also kept a white woman on his arm most of the time. This was definitely not what the white establishment wanted. He traveled abroad extensively and drove flashy cars. This kind of lavish living wasn't intended for blacks, and whites were eager to see this big, black arrogant champion dethroned. If a black was lucky enough to achieve on a "white level," he or she was not supposed to flaunt it, especially in the presence of white people.

Black musicians and athletes continued to make money for white men after slavery, so they were allowed to continue to exist. A white man named Branch Rickey hired Jackie Robinson in 1947 to play baseball for the Brooklyn Dodgers. This single incident probably contributed more to integration in America than anything else.

Musicians were still playing to segregated audiences, but some of them were making sizable amounts of money because they had become popular among blacks and whites (Billie Holiday and Nat King Cole).

White men did not intend for entertainment to be an avenue for blacks to achieve parity, fame, and fortune, but here again greed was the reason it happened. During slavery, black fighters needed to be managed, because bets were made when they fought against each other. Boxers were managed because money was made on the matches. Ballplayers and musicians make a lot of money for a lot of people.

This put some white men in a very precarious situation after slavery because they wanted to keep ex-slaves poor and in their so-called place but they could not resist the urge to make money. They never intended for blacks to earn enough money to be financially equal to white men.

Some blacks were becoming aware of how much they were worth, however, and began to demand a fair price for their performances. Blacks began to dominate the major league sports when they saw that white men would allow them to make money in this area. Blacks would flock to and probably dominate any area where they are allowed to earn according to their ability. Then they could dispel the myth that blacks only can play ball, sing, and dance.

Though black ballplayers were treated cruelly on and off the field, they began to make a better-than-average salary. Blacks were so good and added such spice to the game or show that the public began to demand more of their kind. Competition and greed made other white teams hire blacks, and the fact that integration began to take place was irrelevant to men whose sole interest was in making a buck. The public demand for more became louder, and the opportunities for blacks to earn astronomical amounts of money became greater and greater. Again, many whites did not mean for this to get out of hand, but it did.

Some teams such as the New York Yankees (baseball), the Washington Redskins (football), and the St. Louis Hawks (basket ball) were the last to hire blacks for their teams. The Yankees said they would hire a black if they found one good enough. George Preston Marshall, the owner of the Washington Redskins, supposedly said a black would never play on his team as long as he lived. The St. Louis Hawks players (specifically Cliff Hagen) objected to the black player Cleo Hill being put on the first team, even though he was exceptionally good. They claimed their rational was a player should gradually earn a position on the first team. This had never been a problem before a black came to the team, and it was obvious their objection was to a black being on the team.

In the music world, blacks began to play to bigger black and white audiences. White recording companies and studios began to record more black stars and claimed the biggest part, if not all, of the royalties from recordings of many blacks. While several million dollars were being made for many white people, the black performers also earned a rather lucrative salary.

Blacks no longer dominate the two areas of music and sports, because white American have become acutely aware of the millions of dollars blacks have been deriving from them. Whites are now deciding what is entertainment and who will be doing the entertaining. They are catering to and choosing music (country and western and heavy metal) that blacks are not interested in and sports (soccer, hockey, cycling) to which many blacks have not been exposed.

After earning great sums of money in these fields, these so-called rich blacks for the first time are in a position to help other black Americans. Before this time, blacks who desired to do something about the deplorable situation their people were in were not financially independent enough to make much of a difference. They had to keep quiet and remain obedient to the source from which their finances was derived. Blacks who earned in excess of a million dollars are big enough to make a difference and not be hurt by white people who object to them helping other blacks.

Unfortunately some blacks preferred not to get involved in what they called racial issues. They were apparently ignorant of the fact that they were already involved because they were black. Still others attempted to be colorless and strove hard to be anything in society but black. They moved as far away from blacks as possible in all-white neighborhoods and returned to their old black neighborhood as seldom as possible. Blacks who are in a position to pool together enough finances to save the African American race would much rather expand their efforts and finances in other directions. Feeding their own hungry and clothing their own naked apparently never crosses their mind. Other races definitely help their own first. Jesse Jackson said, "No one will save us but us."

A few blacks (Muhammad Ali, Jim Brown, Bill Russell, Nina Simone, Eartha Kitt, and Paul Robeson) made stands for the black race whenever possible. Blacks have achieved very little along the lines of self-determination, because so few of "dem that's got" share with or lend a hand to their brothers and sisters.

Chapter 36
Muhammad Ali

Cassius Clay was an ambitious young amateur Olympic heavyweight boxer. He captured the minds and hearts of all who watched him box at the 1960 Olympics and went on to become heavyweight champion of the world in 1964. Cassius was a country boy from Louisville, Kentucky, and supposedly for his own protection had several white men who were his handlers. To their and all America's surprise, he became a follower of the Honorable Elijah Muhammad and a disciple of the Islamic religion. He changed his name from Cassius Clay to Muhammad Ali. He dropped all of his white handlers, and Herbert Muhammad, the son of Elijah Muhammad, became his sole handler.

This made white America very angry with the heavyweight champion of the world. He was not only the champion, living in America, but he was also very outspoken and vocal about the racism in America. He was young and good-looking and an excellent boxer. He was surrounded by blacks and controlled by no one. He was rich and famous. He was not interested in acting white and associating with whites. Most of all, he was not interested in dating or marrying a white woman.

Muhammad Ali made another famous stand by not going to fight in the unpopular Vietnam War. He refused to be drafted into the military and said he had no fight with anyone in Vietnam.

This not only infuriated the white establishment; it also opened the eyes of many young Americans whose lives were being sacrificed for a very unclear cause. He made Americans take a look at the wars they were being involved in, and most of all, he pointed out to blacks that they had no real reason to fight a war for America.

In spite of America's effort to save face and induct Ali into the military services, they failed. It cost the champion three years of his great career as a boxer and $2 million, but he stood up for what he believed in and continued to be a Muslim.

Muhammad Ali used his fame and fortune to make a stand for African-Americans. His struggle was virtually futile, however, because of the lack of help he received from other rich and famous blacks.

Chapter 37
The Last Protest

In 1968, the Olympic games were to be held in Mexico City. The black athletes made a historical stand for African-Americans.

Dr. Harry Edwards, a dedicated black activist and coach at San Jose State College, suggested to the black athletes that they boycott the Olympics. He told them that this was their chance to tell the world about the racism blacks were facing in America.

The black athletes who made up the majority of the United States track team were young, uninformed about the subject of white racism, and uninterested in making a stand for black pride. They did not want to give up their chance to make what they considered a personal achievement in America. Some were also being strongly influenced by "handkerchief-headed" coaches, and other white and black people in general. The white American power structure and politicians were certain the black athletes themselves would not band together and make a decision against participating in the Olympics. African-Americans had not made a habit of getting together to make a stand against anything in America.

Jesse Owens, a 1936 black Olympian standout who had been shunned by the supreme racist Adolph Hitler, told the black athletes that they shouldn't even think of not participating in the Olympics in Mexico City. Most other famous blacks either said the same or said nothing.

The president of the United States, Lyndon Johnson, gave his opinion about the potential black boycott. He said in so many words that boycotting the Olympics was the wrong way for black Americans to protest against white racism in America. He intimated that this was their one chance to achieve fortune and international fame and to show patriotism for America. He suggested that they seize the opportunity to be an Olympian. The president further stated that the Olympics wasn't a political event and should not be used to make a political statement. (President Carter saw the Olympics as political and prohibited the U.S. Olympians from participating in the 1980 games in the Soviet Union [the Soviets' invasion of Afghanistan].)

The black athletes attended the 1968 Olympics in Mexico City, and only two of them made a visible stand against white racism in America. John Carlos and Tommie Smith placed first and third in the two hundred-meter-dash, respectively. When they mounted the stands and received their medals and while the Star Spangled Banner was being played, Carlos and Smith raised black gloved clenched fists high above their heads, rather than salute the American flag as was customary.

They stood alone in their protest and purportedly made them selves look bad, rather than America. They were returned to America immediately with no fanfare from blacks or whites. America punished them severely by blackballing them at every opportunity, and sadly enough, many blacks remained silent and Dr. Harry Edwards, John Carlos, and Tommie Smith immediately became obscure Americans.

When black athletes began to use their fame and fortune to protest against white racism in America, whites, who were still in control of the capital, retaliated. Since the 1968 Olympics, very few have recognized that America has made sure that the majority of its Olympians are not blacks. Whereas blacks practically dominated professional sports for a while, in some cases white Americans displayed their dissatisfaction with this by not attending the games. When key positions were no longer manned by whites or a team had a majority of black players, some white people, who make up the majority of the spectators (because they have most of the capital), demanded a change. Blacks have mostly been first team players since the Olympics. They are either superstars or nothing. Whites who can be second string often are not as good as a black player who has been released.

In other words, blacks are being phased slowly out of professional sports in numerous ways. They are being cut off from the places where professional athletes come from-high schools and colleges. Blacks can't afford the price of college anymore, and affirmative action, which formerly gave a black a chance to compete with a white who has had all of the opportunities, no longer exist in many institutions. Black athletes are scrutinized more closely now, and those whom they feel are apt to cause a problem in the future are often cut off at the pass. White America would rather settle for less and lose with a white team than have a black team and win.

Blacks are enjoying their last great years in professional sports in America. Sports and music made African-Americans, and it appears that it will probably be their downfall.

Chapter 38
Racism, the Inevitable in America

Racism is inevitable in America by virtue of the fact that white people are in power in America. Most whites can remain in power and financially secure without the help of black people; therefore, they see little need to liberate blacks or change their racist attitude toward them. Some feel it would be ludicrous for whites to help the descendants of slaves to be as powerful in America as they are.

Blacks are still controlled by a white racist system in America, because they have a false sense of value and are still suckers for red bandannas and the like. They were lured into slavery with trinkets and false promises. Very little has changed for them since they were brought to these shores.

Racism is still a fact of life with America n blacks. because many refuse to take control of their own destiny. A few crumbs (a house, a car) and surviving on their knees seem to be more important to them than standing up together with dignity. They seem to think that one day everything will be all right or just don't care what happens to the black race.

Most other ethnic groups in America experience the same kind of oppression as blacks in America, but it doesn't affect them the same because while they deal with white racists in everyday life, they keep their mind and soul together by identifying with their own people. Chinese feel no need to be blond; therefore, white people make little or no money from them by selling them various hair products. Chinese like being ChineseAmericans and expend their energy achieving for themselves, their family, and their race. Chinese people for the most part eat rice and love it. This means their food or what they eat poses no real problem for them. They know a full stomach is a full stomach and do not love to eat "high on the hog."

Black people, on the other hand, eat beans out of necessity and dream of eating steaks. They give little thought to the fact that protein is protein no matter what the source. Blacks ride in small cars and look forward to purchasing a "big ride" (a Cadillac or Mercedes). A car that gets you to your destination is what a ride should be all about, especially for those who cannot really afford a high-priced car. White auto dealers definitely have blacks on the hook when it comes to high-priced cars, because they know some black men will see their families go hungry for a big, shiny automobile.

No matter how stupid the so-called style is, some blacks will buy and wear it. They never stop to think that whites design and manufacture clothing, et cetera, with them in mind. Many poor and middle-class whites don't worry about wearing the latest styles. Other so-called ethnic groups who usually wear their own native dress also show little interest in the latest styles. Some blacks wear the latest styles in clothing if they have to go hungry. White fashion designers even design African styles (black native dress) for African-Americans. Here again whites dictate to blacks what they should be about and they accept it because it has the white mark of approval.

Blacks in America have been brainwashed into thinking that one has to crawl before one can walk and the "Lord will make a way somehow." Few if any of them are willing to stop crawling from payday to payday until all blacks can survive together with dignity. They don't realize that there will never be a special time to demand their freedom and equality except now. Yet blacks in America wonder why blacks in South Africa don't make such demands. It is because of the few pennies the seventy thousand out of 23 million are earning. Their freedom and self-esteem are sacrificed for the sake of a few. Why don't a few American blacks stop crawling so all blacks can walk? Because of the few pennies they earn, which continue to give them false hope. They sacrifice the freedom of the majority for the sake of a few cents.

If they could bring themselves to say, "I won't ride in style until all blacks can ride in style," if they could say, "I won't eat steak until all blacks can eat steak," and if they could say, "I won't wear the latest styles until all blacks can wear the latest styles," blacks would gain parity with other races in America at a rapid pace. In South Africa, slavery is called apartheid. It has no official name in America, but blacks must be aware that it still exists.

Blacks have allowed racism to become a crutch and their excuse for not making progress in America. They have become complacent, not realizing the fact that a hopeless situation should not make an individual lose self-pride. Racism does not make one disrespect one's elders. There was a time when blacks respected all old people. Racism did not change this; black people changed this. The very idea that they would show disrespect for their elders and blame racism is ridiculous, to say the least. Vulgarity and self-destruction are usually one's own choosing. Abuse of one's body with alcohol and other drugs is not caused by racism. Blacks could remain free from these habit-forming drugs in spite of racism.

Almost 50 percent of the murders in America are of black people. Most of the murders of blacks are committed by blacks. There was a time when blacks feared being killed by a white man. Now a black man's greatest fear has to be being killed by one of his own race. After slavery was abolished, black men were often wounded in a fight by another black wielding a knife or a bottle. Now that guns are available to blacks and respect for human life is at an all-time low, blacks are killed, not wounded, at little or no provocation. The racist trick of genocide is to hold back jobs and make drugs and alcohol accessible so blacks will get rid of each other. The tragic part of it all is that blacks still fall for the trick.

When a black is killed, it is still a routine event, especially when a black kills another black. Black on black crime has always been routine in America. Black on white crime is investigated thoroughly and with fervor. This is racist and biased, and the people who advocate this system arc no less than murderers themselves.

As a result of racism, blacks still do not have confidence in other blacks. When a black is given a raw deal by whites, he goes to another white. When a black is given a raw deal by a black, he says, "I should've known better than to've gone to dat nigger in the first place." They never consider the fact that the reason they receive so many raw deals from blacks is because blacks won't deal with blacks enough for them to become proficient in any given area. Whites won't deal with blacks and blacks won't deal with blacks, making it impossible for blacks to make normal progress. Blacks have been taught through the years that blacks' merchandise is inferior, not why blacks' merchandise is often inferior. Now most blacks thoroughly believe blacks' goods are inferior, even if the blacks' merchandise is the same as the whites'. Therefore most blacks deal exclusively with whites, to the detriment of the few black merchants who struggle to exist. Older blacks say it's too late for them to change and feel change is up to the young folks. Young blacks who have so-called integrated into the white educational system in America don't know or care about changing the situation of blacks in America. Young blacks relate to the fact that it appears to be a luxury to be as white as they can be. Their parents have taught them nothing different, and they certainly didn't learn anything different in the white schools they attended.

One reason many whites will never change their racist attitude toward blacks in America is because they don't know anything else. Blacks were brought to America to be slaves forever. When blacks were set free, this posed an immediate problem for whites that has not been solved to this day. Now, in everything that white America endeavors, the question of "what about the blacks?" is always imminent.

Whites capitalized on the fact that blacks didn't own anything when they were so-called freed and would have to come to them for everything, just as they did when they were in slavery. Good or bad, this has worked for them throughout the years, and they are afraid lo chance changing it for blacks' sake.

White racists' greatest accomplishment in this area was making blacks think there was hope for them in a virtually hopeless situation. They enslaved blacks for all of those years, kept them ignorant of the language, and deprived them of the opportunity to achieve in America, yet they say, "They can make it if they try." They even make the black who is the victim look like the villain when he doesn't make it, which is more times than not. Blacks, especially the few who think they are making it, will also say, "Dem niggers could make it if they'd get off their ass." They are concerned about making progress as an individual in America rather than as a race, which is virtually impossible. In order to have clout in the world, one must identify with a nation. Most black Americans refuse to identify with the nations of Africa; therefore, they have no clout and no nationalism.

White racists like to point to blacks who have so-called "made it" in America. Unfortunately, all blacks are not musically and/or athletically inclined. Blacks have dominated these areas to the point that whites are reluctant to open other fields to them, knowing their need to achieve. They are totally oblivious to the fact that keeping blacks out of medical school may be the reason there is no cure for cancer. Only the most ignorant of the white race still believe the brains of whites are superior to the brains of blacks.

Consistent racism in America has forced blacks to take a backseat in most professional areas, and many blacks can no longer afford the tuitions required to attend medical school and law schools. At this point, if things go true to form, if and when the cure for cancer is discovered, it will be by a white man-- either that or people throughout the world will be allowed to continue to suffer with and die of cancer.

Another factor that blacks have to contend with in the majority of American cities is a Ku Klux Klan mentality. Even blacks who have apparently made it are viewed as "niggers" in the eyes of many white Americans.

A black doctor is mostly seen as a "black doctor" and patronized mostly by blacks. White men do not want their wives, mothers, and/or sisters to be attended to by a black doctor.

A black who is a lawyer in most American cities is seen as a "black lawyer" by blacks and whites and seldom, if ever, allowed to become a member of corporate law firms, where the big money is.

Black movie stars make black movies no matter how many whites participate in the movie with them. White movies are viewed by all as just movies, whereas in many cases whites do not really patronize movies that blacks star in. Black movies are black movies, advertised as such for the most part, stereotyped as such, distributed as such, and viewed by mostly black people. Whites only watch black comedians on television and in movies, and they must remain funny to remain on screen. Whites are not interest in blacks playing roles as ordinary men and women in everyday life; therefore, black children seldom, if ever, see black role models to pattern themselves after when they attend movies or watch television.

White people in power force many ethnic peoples to take degrading roles that are racist and damaging. Black children viewing whites in serious and powerful roles see a true picture of America, but they also see an ugly image of their own race.

Strangely enough, blacks still laugh at themselves and the Strangely enough, blacks still laugh at themselves and the plight of the black man in America. They allow jokes to be told on or about them even in their presence. Blacks who feel they have made it think it is in vogue to tell or share a "black joke" with their white colleagues. Yet they would never tell a joke about a person of another ethnic background in the person's presence. This means some blacks respect other so-called ethnic races more than they do their own.

Blacks in America also display more concern for others with problems than they do their own. They sympathized with the Jews when President Reagan visited Bitberg, where German Nazi soldiers were buried. They protested against apartheid in South Africa readily, but apparently condone segregation in America. White racists who allowed blacks to be castrated. boiled in oil, and murdered outright are celebrated in many cases by whites and blacks.

Most blacks will not admit and choose to ignore the fact that things have not really changed that much for blacks in America. There are still places in every town and city in America where blacks are not wanted or actually cannot go in spite of the civil rights laws that have been passed.

Many people, black and white, in the larger cities in America think that outright racism does not continue to exist. Most of America is made up of small towns and cities, however, not big, impersonal cities. This is not to say that racism does not exist in big cities in America. Racism is well camouflaged in big cities, but blacks are aware it is there.

In small towns and cities, racism and segregation are practiced openly and blatantly. There are in man y towns a group of so-called rednecks and good old boys making all of the decisions. Some of them wear shirts and ties, and some of them wear overalls. They all have one thing in common, and that is a dislike for a "nigger." They live in the same neighborhood, belong to the same country club, and attend the same church. The "good old boys" sip coffee and liquor in the same places and figure out how to keep the "niggers" from sharing the same privileges as they do under the law. Blacks, with all of their hope and energy, cannot help make policy in small towns run by whites, because they are not invited to drink coffee and liquor after hours. All of the marching, praying, voting, and dying will make little or no difference. The rules are changed daily and nightly by the town judge, lawyer, doctor, and preacher, who all vote the same way. This is the way it is in small racist towns all over America, and blacks know this all too well. All blacks in large cities know how to act when they go back home down south, out west, up north, and back east.

Rebel flags denoting the racist attitude of whites can be seen all over America. They have been displayed so much that even blacks who are ignorant of the flag and its significance often display them on their cars, clothing, et cetera. This symbol of racism has been a part of America for so long that it is ignored by blacks, but definitely not by whites who continue to identify with it.

The slogan "America, love it or leave it" was originated at the same time blacks were protesting against America's racist policies in the sixties. Here again, blacks can be seen with this slogan on their T-shirt, car bumpers et cetera. This means, of course, that racism has become such a way of life in America that the ones it was intended to keep down, practice it themselves out of ignorance.

Ironically enough, blacks are so dependent upon the same men who held them in captivity for four hundred years that they still need his help to free themselves. This is true only because they never freed their minds after slavery was abolished. The slave master took the chains from the slaves' legs and placed them on their brains. They stifled blacks' ability to make decent lives for themselves like others in the so-called melting pot in America and point the finger at them while they struggle.

Institutionalized racism in America has kept blacks in the mud throughout the years. When one black is able to pull himself out of the mud, he is expected to immediately get a shower on his own and remain as groomed as whites who have never been in the mud. He is not supposed to have any remembrance of the mud puddles he left behind and is expected to compete in a country that keeps reminding him that he is not as good as others because he came from the mud.

When they are not successful, blacks arc led to believe they didn't vote right or didn't work hard enough. When blacks are playing the white man's game in America, it is virtually impossible for them to win, especially when the white man makes all of the rules and changes them daily to be sure he always wins.

Whites always have the last word inasmuch as they hold the purse strings. If a black wins on any level, whites either own him or cut off the funds. Jesse Jackson proved to all that a black had a right to run for the office of president of the United States. It was ludicrous, however, to think the big-money people of America would allow him to actually become the president of this country. If he had won, then what? Except for pride, blacks derive few benefits from another black being in a high position, because he or she is almost always manipulated by the white power structure. Like in the big cities with black mayors, the white men with all of the money pull the strings and the black "winner" becomes a puppet.

Blacks have allowed racism and the lack of finances to keep them from making progress in America. Whites who control blacks' destinies by controlling the purse strings have made sure that they remain subservient and out of the mainstream of America. This has continued to be true over the years, because blacks have no unity of ideas. Invariably, no matter in what part of the country a black finds himself, he is expected to know his place and remain in it. Many whites seem to think they know where a black's place is in America and if blacks don't remain in their place, whites will put them in it one way or another. Racists accomplish this mostly by blocking blacks' opportunities to make progress in the job world. In many cases this is done in such a subtle way in America that few realize it and no one, even blacks, seems to bother about fighting it anymore.

A few blacks like Muhammad Ali, Malcolm X, Jesse Jackson, and others, have gotten "out of place" recently, but this gave white America the opportunity to teach the entire black American population a lesson. They defeated them and their purpose handily, and many blacks helped them. Blacks help them put outspoken blacks in their place, because they too have been programmed into the white racist way of thinking.

Racism will be present in America as long as there are black people in America and white people in America. It would seem that blacks would be keenly aware of this by now and would be doing something constructive about it. If dying for the right to vote, educating themselves, getting lighter skin and longer hair, and acting white hasn't changed things in the last hundred years, it seems blacks would be ready to try something else.

Blacks may not be doing something about the problem of blacks in America, but whites are. Black people sit idly by while their whole race is slowly escaping from them. They talk about genocide in a blase manner as though it is not really happening to them. They also have barely noticed their children, whom they have sent to the better white schools and have been thoroughly indoctrinated by well-trained white teachers (or white-thinking black teachers who no longer think black). Young black children are the future of the black race, and they don't know about blackness nor do they seem to care about blackness. They talk like white people, they think like white people, they dress like white people, they sing like white people, and. believe it or not, they even dance like white people. This is not Just happening to the young blacks; older blacks are allowing it to happen to them also. Blacks continue, after more than one hundred years of so-called freedom, to cater to the light-skinned, straight-haired black, and of course whites are capitalizing on this. Whites and blacks still require more in every walk of life from the dark-skinned, kinky-haired black. Therefore this true African-American is rapidly becoming extinct.

Thanks to some very skillful inventors, they have discovered a way to take the kinks out of any African-American's hair (Jerry Curl or S Curl). The few blacks left who choose to wear their hair natural will not be able to hold out much longer, because neither the black nor white society will tolerate it much longer. Dreadlocks are out of the question. Few jobs are available to kinky-haired blacks, because they no longer look groomed to blacks and/or whites in hiring positions. Since these kind of people determine who is hired, it becomes expedient that a black seeking a certain job looks like the kind of people that are being hired.

Inventors have also discovered a makeup that makes all blacks look red or some other color besides black. No matter how dark a black is, the colored eye shadow and the red makeup make him look like something besides a black.

Since the bottom line seems to be economics, blacks are rapidly losing their identity. If the white man who has the jobs and does the hiring and firing decides what a black should look like before he will hire him or her, then blacks will do their damndest to look the part. "He who pays the piper names the tunes."

For a black man to be accepted, in many cases he must be thin, wear a three-piece suit, straighten his hair, act somewhat. effeminate, and show no interest in white females. It helps to have been trained in a white institution; this way, he will know most of the rules. This is the kind of black man that is being hired on the decent jobs today, and, believe it or not, many blacks are doing the hiring. They know what kind of black man their white boss man will accept and if they don't hire this type, they too will be seeking employment. Black men who insist upon looking like the kinky-haired, rugged black of old will not find themselves in an office making lots of money, no matter what degree they possess.

The black man was previously the center of the family structure. When black men could no longer earn a living adequate lo maintain their families, it was the beginning of the end for black families. When black women ceased to respect black men for what they were rather than what they earned, it was all over for the black family. The fact that a woman was a schoolteacher and a man a farmer was not a problem in the black family before Women's Liberation was introduced to black women. Black women had a man in the house and respecting him along with the children, in spite of his earning power. The white man never intended for a black man to be respected in America by anyone (especially the white woman) because of the amount of money he earned. When the black man lost the respect of the black woman and his children, he became the dumping ground for all America. The white man would have Americans believe black men have always been nothing, like he has them believing Indians want to be on reservations, poor and hungry. The black man was the head of his family from Africa to Women's Liberation. "Kill the head and the body is sure to die." Black families will soon be a thing of the past.

So, though racism is the inevitable in America, it won't be necessary for black people to do anything about this. In fact, there will be no need for racism in America, because soon, and very soon, blacks will no longer be black; they will be white.

"If you don't know where you are going, any road will take you there and any man can take you there. If you don't know who you are, then you are anybody and nobody." Blacks should take a good look at their race, because it will soon be a thing of the past.

Just because racism is inevitable in America does not mean blacks have to continue to be victims of racism. They will be the victims as long as they allow themselves to be. Jesse Jackson said, "No one will save us but us."

Yes, blacks shall overcome-not if a civil rights bill is passed, not if a voters' rights bill is passed, not if it is the Lord's will, but only if they want to overcome bad enough to join forces and make the sacrifices necessary to be recognized as people in America, their home.

Poems and Articles by Edward Faison, Jr.

Y'all C'mon Home and Buy Freedom

Brothers and sisters, y'all may as well c'mon home.
Folks down here talkin' 'bout buying freedom.
Yeah . . . I know ya jes' had ta go up north ta see if ya could better yoself.
Well . . . y'all dun seed thangs ain't no better

and ya never should've left.

So why don't ya jes c'mon home?

Ain't ya tard of faking it, lack Stevie Wonder said,
"Livin' jes' 'nuff fer da city," sometimes wid no bread.
Makin' like life is some kind a bowl of cherries, livin' from hand ta mouth.
Y'all may as well c'mon back home...

What's wrong wid da south?

Dey got television, McDonald's, ain't got no numbers but ya can bet, If enuff colored folks come down here they'll get some... don't you fret.
Dey don't care how much dem church folk grumbles. White folks know colored folk gotta have dem numbers.

Up yonder, ya spend most of da time going to work and coming back home.
All dem folks up der ... and ya still alone.
Ain't even no need ta have no car,
Wid dem potholes, no parking spaces, and not knowing where ya are.
'Sides dat, dey always stealin' da cars up der

Runnin' dared lights . . . don't nobody care.
Scared ta go back out once ya chained and locked in.
What kinda place is dat fer yo' chilluns? . . . Oughtto beasin.
Call everybody ya know on da phone . . . dat is if ya gota phone.
Even crosstown is long distance ... so ya can't talk long.

So what I'm trying ta tell y'all is, day got all dem thangs down here

Even got families wid men in 'em, and da women ain't got no fear.
Ole folk ain't in prison in der apartments, and da kids don't run da school.
In fact, most of da folk down here live by da Golden Rule.

Say, fo 'ya know it, ya gon be on da take yoself.
Den you'll be in trouble and wish ya never hadda left.
You better c'mon back home.

Ya see, when our folks got freed, dey ain't had no place ta go.
No land, no home—dey jes' wasn't slaves no mo.
But white folks acted lack dey wasn't even free.
Still treated colored folks bad, so dey had to flee.
Wouldn't even let dem congregate.
Po' colored folk didn't know how much mo' dey could take.
When dey stopped dem from settin' up over da dead and going ta church at night,
Oat wuz it, 'cause ya know how dey wuz 'bout dem funeral rites.
Dey got tagether and decided it wuz time fer dem ta leave from down here.
Singing and shoutin', colored folks went everywhere.
White folk had vested in dem lack dey had dey home.
Didn't make no difference, though 'ca use dcm colored folk wuz gon.

So dey went up north where dey thought dey'd be safe.
Somebody'd done told dem dey could stay anyplace.
Oat wuz a shame what dey came back here and done.
Gold teeth and rented cars and claiming day wuz having so much fun.
Sweared out dey wuz doing good up yonder.

Lying 'bout dem white girls and da hundred-dollar bills dey had squandered.
Dey right den had on clothes dey had borrowed fer free
But folks back here couldn't wait ta get up north and see.
Y' all better quit jivin' and c'mon back here, where der ain't no pollution
And da weather is good and clear.

Don't even hardly need no heavy coat, 'cuz da snow don't las' no time.
Ain't nobody on dat ole dope, and der ain't even much of dat der wine.

Folk down here give ya all da vegetables ya can eat.
Can't help from getting fat, 'cause dey cook so many sweets.
White folks is north, south, east, and west.
Wherever dey is ya know der ain't no rest.
No jobs, no houses, not even no hoe...
Least down here thangs ain't fast dey slow.

We need y'all down here, 'cause dey's takin our land lack mad.
Y'all know our land is all dat we had.
White man love it, 'cause it ain't costin' him a dime.
If y'all come back, it could be us 'stead of him all da time.

Look, I know some of y'alls doing pretty good and don't want ta come back home.
But think of da rest of us and get wid dis here—buy freedom.
We could get tagether jes' fer us fer a change.
Tony Brown said if we buy freedom, we stand ta gain.

Long time ago, we had ta buy freedom 'cause we couldn't do much else.
Seems ta me we wuz doing better den.

Now ya besides yoself.

I know ya jes can't drop everything and come down here.
But think about it, tell ya chilluns 'bout it; fer God's sake don't jes' sit dere.
Don't let dem thank dey's trapped up der in dat jungle and can't go noplace.
We's already losin' our families, so ain't no time ta waste.

1 b'lieve if we can git dis buy-freedom ta workin' fer us, We gonna find ourselves . . . ain't got no choice. . .
Ain't nobody in da White House we can trust.
So think about dis and let's help each other some.
And c'mon back down here and buy freedom.

A Message to African-Americans[1*]

Would anyone mind if I wrote something different for this Black History Month?

We have given people, especially our black children, the same black heroes for so long that many of them think stories about Fredrick Douglass, Harriet Tubman, Martin Luther King, Jr., et cetera, are fairy tales. They can look forward to the same posters, stories, and movie s being shown, then placed back in storage without having any real impact on anyone, black or white.

Would anyone mind if I attempted to give black people another dimension or a new story this February?

I would like to write on the effect "the peculiar institution" of slavery in America had on African-American people. First of all, it was apparently so effective and devastating that many blacks in America choose to act as though it never really took place. It has had this kind of lasting effect even after more than one hundred years of so-called freedom. Though American blacks still feel the results of their having been enslaved and are faced with its scars even now, they prefer to keep silent about it. Jewish people keep the Holocaust in the forefront of our minds. They say it is necessary in order to be sure it never happens to a people again.

When you take on the home of your enslaver without reservations or alterations, you are truly enslaved. (Think about it.)

Many blacks in America tend to shield their children from stories of their past because they are bitter and distasteful. Yet they will allow them to attend movie s and deal with distorted versions of what happened to us, told by people who continue to exploit and make money from our past. Few tell the story of

---

*Originally published in the Carolinian. Used by permission.

the Jews' past but the Jews. Most of all, they do not allow their oppressor to tell their story.

"The peculiar institution" was the name given to the form of slavery practiced in America by the slave holders. It was called such because it was the only time in the history of any slavery that a slaves name, culture, identity, and homeland were taken away from him. The slave owners knew that if they took away the Africans' past, they would eventually offer little or no opposition to being enslaved. Apparently, after several hundred years of brainwashing, many blacks in America have no idea who they are or how they came to be the so-called unwanted Americans. Worse yet, some American blacks still refuse to face the truth about their real status here in America. Until they are able to deal with this fact, they will never be able to change anything about their situation. Any black who doesn't wish to change his or her status in America has not realized the truth about himself in America. Most of them refuse to deal with revolution because they think it means violence. Revolution simply means change. Yet the same blacks are reaping the benefits from the struggles and sacrifices others have made since slavery and continue to make.

Someone said, "If you don't know where you're going, any road will take you there." If you don't know who you are, then anyone can control your destiny. Give me your mind and I'll tell you where to go.

Most Americans are a part of the so-called American Melting Pot, but proudly identify with their native land or motherland, even if they have never set foot on its soil. Chinese are Chinese Americans, Italians are Italian Americans, Greeks are Greek Americans, et cetera—native land first, America second. Jewish people all over the world say, "We won!" when Israel wins a battle.

Though blacks have never really melted into the so-called American Melting Pot, they cannot be accused of not having tried. They have gone so far as to bleach their skin and hair to be accepted. African-Americans are in a very precarious situation here because, yes, they are Americans and, yes, they do belong here. The problem is, they are in America but not necessarily of America. No, they are not from Africa and, no, they don't belong in Africa. So, no, they can't go back to Africa. They can and should identify with Africa, however, the home of their ancestors, and recognize it as their native land. This gives them "roots," which are necessary for growth for anything and anyone. Besides, they don't have any other country to identify with. Most American blacks do not wish to identify with Africa. They wouldn't dare refer to themselves as African-Americans because of the thorough brainwashing that took place during slavery.

How do you become accepted in a country where you are not welcomed, that you did not choose to be your home, and where you are restricted simply because of the color of your skin? This is a very difficult question that may never be answered. One thing blacks in America can do, however, is face the realization as to where they came from, who they are, and where they are going. This may at least help them cope. with the precarious situation they have been placed in here in this country.

Remember "The Negro National Anthem"—true to our God, true to our native land? Could it be our forefathers (James Weldon Johnson and his brother) knew something we didn't know? Did they know that Africa is the richest continent in the world? Corporations in South Africa know this. Did they know that Africa is the second largest continent in the world? It is the most beautiful continent in the world and is three times as large as the United States. He who controls Africa controls the world. The United States and the Soviet Union know this. All African descendants should know these things.

Black History Month should not necessarily dwell on things that happened after the signing of the Emancipation Proclamation or those people who struggled for freedom and recognition during and after slavery. Black people, especially the youngsters, should and must know there was a time when black people were free and prosperous.

They must know that Egypt is in Africa. They must be taught that Tutankhamen (King Tut) an Egyptian king of the eighteenth dynasty was a real African king, not an exhibition of gold. They must be taught that Africans built the great pyramids and the Sphinx of Egypt, wonders of the world that have stood for thousands of years. Black History Month should teach that the pharaohs were great rulers of Egypt, rich and intelligent, rather than bad men who were merely persecutors of the Israelites. Black people must know that Ethiopia was the center of civilization, not the center of starvation.

With this kind of knowledge and information, black people might have the motivation to help themselves. Jesse Jackson said, "No one will save us but us."

So before African-Americans take for granted they will just one day melt into America's Melting Pot and be plain Americans, they should think again. As was stated previously, ethnic groups in America identify with their native countries. I would like to inform black people in America that there is no "Blackland," there is no "Negroland," there is no "Coloredland," and there is no "Niggerland." Therefore they can derive no nationalism or respect by identifying with any of these titles.

Most American blacks, especially the younger ones, ask how our ancestors allowed someone to take them into slavery. The question to black people now is, how they allow someone to keep their minds in slavery. During slavery, the only thing a slave could possibly hold onto was his mind, even if, in fact, he was strong-willed. Where is your mind now, African-American people, now that you are supposed to be free? Have they taken the chains from your ankles and placed them on your brain? The saying is, "No chains and prisons bars can hold you; it's your mind that controls you."

Has anyone thought that African-American history should be taught daily as is American history, rather than one month out of the year? African-American history is not a state of one race's mind, but a fact of life in America.

Blacks' Prayer for Thanksgiving*

Blacks' prayer for Thanksgiving should have nothing to do with the Pilgrims and how they survived during their early days here in this country. They should spend this holiday reflecting on how they themselves have survived and continue to survive in America under such adverse circumstances.

No matter what the Reagan administration says, black people in America today are having it hard. According to up-to-date statistics, more than half the black population is out of work. We all know that statistics usually only tell half the story. This means there are a lot of people depending on food stamps for food. Contrary to what many people may believe, it is hard to feed a family for a month with the few food stamps allotted per person at Social Services.

Many blacks don't realize the trouble they are in because they have always had it tough. There has never really been a time throughout the history of blacks in America when everything was all right. Jobs have never been plentiful, opportunities have never been plentiful, and stumbling blocks have never been moved from the paths of blacks in America. Yet many blacks will find the time to pray for the Pilgrims on Thanksgiving.

Blacks have only recently felt the pangs of a depression, because they have recently been led to believe they are a part of middle-class America. The so-called middle class people lose during a depression because they are the working people. These are the people who keep the economy going by spending money on cars and houses.

Since slavery was abolished, a few blacks, with a great deal of struggling, have made a little progress here in America. The majority of blacks are only two paydays away from poverty. A sudden illness, an untimely death, and/or a loss of employment would set them back for life. Besides a car and a house, most blacks have little or nothing to show for their struggles.

For many years after slavery, blacks were compelled to work together to save each other. After integration and a few so-called opportunities, blacks no longer felt the need to be their "brothers' keeper." Black churches that were the backbones of all black neighborhoods no longer feed the hungry and clothe the naked. Instead, they pay enormous salaries and have become places where friends meet to show off the latest fashions.

Like all other so-called ethnic groups, African-Americans must know that the welfare of their people is their responsibility. Our black people are doomed if we are to continue to depend on the government for welfare, because one has to "be poor to get on it and stay poor to stay on it."

African-Americans must know that they cannot outgrow or escape their heritage. Therefore it would be most expedient that they do all they can to make things better from within their race. "Birds of a feather flock together." One should never abandon one's own. No other race does. This is not to say that African Americans should not have love for the human race. It simply means that you clean up your own house first and then go and help clean up your neighbor's house. "Self-preservation is the first law of nature."

Finally, there are those blacks who are willing to leave their fate entirely up to the Lord. I believe we are the only people who leave our fate entirely up to the Lord. Someone said, "The Lord helps those who help themselves." We blacks must join hands and help ourselves.

For black people, Jesse Jackson said, "No one will save us but us." Think about it.

The focus should be on you first no matter what holiday it is. Blacks' prayer for Thanksgiving should be for blacks.

Should African-Americans Dislike Moammar Khadafy?

Should African-Americans dislike Moammar Khadafy because our white American leaders tell us to? Whose side are AfricanAmericans supposed to be on? Libya is in Africa, and Mr. Khadafy is an African. Are African-Americans supposed to support Africa and Africans, or do they owe their allegiance to America?

Why shouldn't black Americans like Moammar Khadafy? He is handsome and cool, dresses well, and seems to be a shrewd politician. These are the traits we have been taught as Americans to admire in men. These are the kind of politicians we elect to run our country.

African-Americans are very familiar with terrorism. They have been victims of terrorism since the day they were snatched from their motherland, Africa, and enslaved in this faraway land called America. We still bear scars from white terrorists, who continue to attack us in many ways and places all over these United States. The Ku Klux Klan has existed openly and actively in America since 1865, to the objection of few white people. Acts of terrorism toward black Americans continue to be prevalent in America, because blacks are still poor and hungry, are still denied equal opportunity, and are still looked upon as second-class citizens. Blacks in America are in just as bad or worse shape as they were fifty years ago. Why should black Americans support America over Africa? Because of a racist mentality that continues to exist in America, aJl of the singing, praying, begging, and dying blacks have done has not changed much for them. Blacks in America face racism daily and have virtually nothing to look forward to but more of the same. Why should blacks pledge their allegiance to the same country and the same people who continue to treat them like slaves?

This dates back to when black children were taught in Sunday school that the pharaohs in Egypt were bad men. I rejoiced along with all of the other little black children when we were taught that "pharaoh's army got drowned" and the Israelites crossed to the other side of the Red Sea triumphantly. We were not told that the pharaohs were great African rulers. We didn't even know Egypt was in Africa.

I hated Hitler, Mussolini, and the Japanese because I was told to do so during World War II. We were told by our white leaders that they were our enemies. I hated Germans and Italians when I didn't even know they were white, just like the German Americans, and Italian-Americans. This left me really hating the only enemy that was visible-the Japanese. White American leaders decided it was safer to imprison the Japanese-Americans because they might side with their mother country. Why aren't our leaders afraid blacks in America will side with Africa and Moammar Khadafy? I did not know during World War II that the Japanese were people of color. I should have known, when I saw where white America dropped the bomb.

When Fidel Castro came to the United Nations meeting held in New York in the fifties, he stayed in the Theresa Hotel. This was a black hotel located in Harlem, owned and operated by blacks. Blacks in America laughed at Mr. Castro's not knowing he was identifying with them. We were told by our white leaders that Fidel Castro was a "bearded fool" and we dared not identify with him because he was supposedly anti-American. We were not told that Cubans were people of color who were struggling to free themselves and determine their own destiny.

Korean and Vietnamese soldiers asked black American soldiers why they were fighting a war for America. Black soldiers were hard pressed for an answer, because they had been thoroughly brainwashed. Korean and Vietnamese soldiers told black soldiers they had no fight with soldiers who had skin that the same color as theirs.

Black soldiers were asked to go to Grenada and kill their own brothers last year. White American leaders had blacks and Indians singing "God Bless America" and saluting the American flag while more than half their people were poor, hungry, and unemployed.

I find it difficult to dislike Mr. Khadafy just because he does not bow down to President Reagan and Secretary of State Schultz. I see them as warmongers attempting to control all of the world that the Soviet Union doesn't control. They do not condemn President Marcos and the terrorism in the Philippines that they finance and support. The Shah of Iran was the number one terrorist of his nation and was financed and supported by America and the same people who condemn Khadafy.

I admire Moammar Khadafy's nerve in standing up against these so-called world leaders and telling them they are the real terrorists and they had been terrorizing the world Jong before he came into power. He recognized the political game that America and Russia play with the world and refuses to participate.

It is not for me to determine at this time who the real villains are. I feel I should be like other ethnic Americans and pledge my allegiance to Africa and Africans. Nobody condemns American Jews who side with Israel, a country that terrorizes wherever and whenever they please. American Jews openly support Mr. Sharon even though his terrorist acts caused the deaths of many innocent people. The important issue here is that Jews identify with their motherland and their countrymen. Other ethnic Americans identify with their mother country first and America second.

Most of all, white Americans support each other, no matter how vicious the crime or terrorist act, especially when the issue is white versus black.

Blacks in America, on the other hand, are expected not to support Africa and/or Africans such as Mr. Khadafy, former Ugandan leader Idi Amin, and even in some instances South

African Bishop Tutu and Mrs. Winnie Mandela. We dare not openly admire PLO leader Yasser Arafat, former Black Nationalists leader Malcolm X, and most certainly not the Muslim minister Farrakhan.

I admire Moammar Khadafy because he is of my own image. I have been asked by my oppressors to pledge allegiance to a flag that has meant nothing but blood, sweat, and tears to African Americans and many other people of color. I have been taught to worship a God that is not in my image, who supposedly created the most racist people in the world today.

Whose side should African-Americans be on? In the words of the Negro National Anthem: "Shadowed beneath thou hand, may we forever stand, true to our God, true to our native land."

About Martin Luther King, Jr.'s Birthday

It's up to the people, especially the black people, not to let greedy merchants turn the celebration of Martin Luther King, Jr.'s birthday into a commercial fiasco. The holidays we celebrate now for the most part are days that you need extra money to buy gifts (Christmas, Easter, and Mother's Day). The merchants use the media and everything available to them to make sure holidays continue to be a time to spend money.

Dr. King was not about money and things that money can buy. He was a Nobel Peace Prize winner. There can be little or no peace where money is the main concern, as it is with most of the other holidays. As happened with Christmas and Easter, the true meaning of peace on earth and freedom will soon be forgotten if we allow Martin Luther King Day to be commercialized.

Dr. King was about loving, caring, and sharing. I believe we should spend his holiday loving, caring, and sharing just like he did while he was here with us. We should be concerned with educating our people and the world about Martin Luther King, Jr., and his commitment to nonviolence. He was amongst the greatest of the orators, and his messages are well worth remembering.

Unfortunately, there are children, black and white, in America who think Dr. King was just another black man that dreamed he would one day enjoy equal rights with the white race. It is sad but true that most black people allow their heroes to be passed over and forgotten as though they were fictitious characters.

Though Martin Luther King Day should not necessarily be thought of as a black holiday, it is true that it came about because of a black man who had blacks and poor people in mind. Certainly, Dr. King died defending the rights of all people who were deprived of their freedom and peace.

If Martin Luther King, Jr., was truly the people's hero, the government should not have h d to declare his birthday a holiday. In the fashion of Dr. King, the people should have demonstrated their love and respect for him by taking off in spite of their jobs and other commitments. Jews take off on Jewish holidays no matter who or what. Dr. King believed in people doing things they thought were right in spite of restrictions. This would have been a tribute to his greatness in a spirit that he would have appreciated. Now that the holiday has been given to the people, it is up to them to decide how Dr. King should be commemorated.

I believe we should celebrate this holiday in the fashion the brother Martin died, campaigning for righteousness and doing something to help others. As on New Year's Eve, people should make resolutions—to treat others better no matter their race, creed, or color.

I believe Dr. King, who said he would like to be remembered as "a drum major for justice, righteousness, and peace," would feel he did not give his life in vain if people of all nationalities would come together in spirit and in song on his holiday.

Again it is up to the people not to let the celebration of this holiday be about money, but about love.

I Still Like Jesse Jackson, But ...

I still like Jesse Jackson, but when I see him way overseas in those foreign countries, I feel so distant from him and somewhat different about him. I don't feel like he is "my man" and that he belongs to us like he used to. His scope seems to have widened to the point that I can hardly remember what he was originally about, and I wonder if he knows what he is really about now. I wish he would come back to earth and to us and get with the grass-roots again.

I don't know if it has occurred to Mr. Jackson or not, but many country preachers leave their small hometowns, churches, and environments, for whatever reason or reasons, and lose the focus of their original premise. Down south we call it "getting too big for your britches." They become engrossed with other matters and seldom, if ever, regain the focus. Some even forget "from whence they came" and lose sight on the world.

Mr. Jackson made exceptional achievements in many areas and certainly has gone as far or further than any other black man in America. Fortunately, he is still young and handsome and has his good health and a stable family. I hope he doesn't push his luck too far, because white racist America has a way of destroying black men who do exceptionally well in America in spite of them.

Mr. Jackson was involved in the sit-ins in Greensboro, he was a part of the movement led by Martin Luther King, Jr., he heads P.U.S.H. for Excellence and ran for the office of the president of the United States of America. He is truly a dynamic speaker. Every time I have had the honor of being in Mr. Jackson's presence or hearing him speak, I got chills and goose pimples, because I felt I was in the presence of a great black man. I got this feeling with another great black man, Muhammad Ali, and I watched him go from the apex of excellence to what appears now to be mediocrity—mostly because he achieved his greatness in spite of white America.

Martin Luther King, Jr., based himself in the South, where black people seemed to have needed him most. No matter where he went, he identified with and returned to the South, where the people were his stronghold. Unlike Martin Luther King, Jr., Mr. Jackson visit the South occasionally, but he does not pallicularly identify himself with the South and southern people. He seems to think of the world as his base and does not seem to have any particular stronghold, though he supposedly caters to the poor and the needy. Martin Luther King, Jr., was our man, and there was no doubt in our minds whose side he was on.

It is time for Jesse to regroup. When you have gone as far as you can go, unfortunately the only things you can do is come down. If coming back to us is coming down, then he will be coming down with the folks who helped him get up there in the first place. We will let him down easy.

Jesse's star was shining brightest when he made the speech at the Democratic convention. He covered all bases and made the greatest speech most of us have ever heard. I feel he will never be able to top himself, especially in the political arena. Besides, white people have a way of being prepared for a black on the "second go-round."

Mr. Jackson has proven himself to Americans and the world. He overcame all of the adversities he faced and established himself as a statesman. He has shown blacks that they too have the ability and can run for the top office in the United States. We know that the only thing "wrong" with him is the color of his skin. There is no reason for him to continue to follow the crowds, repeating himself and "crying in the wilderness." I wish he wouldn't spread himself so thin, apparently searching for a purpose until he becomes vulnerable and lose his credibility.

Black people still love him, though many didn't have the gumption to vote for him. We should have declared him our official leader and president in spite of the outcome of the presidential election. We still need a leader and would appreciate it very much if Mr. Jackson would leave those unsolvable world problems to Reagan and the other warmongers of the world. I know Mr. Jackson would like to be an international peacemaker, but Greensboro and Greenville and hungry black people all over America need him.

I can assure him if he will return to us, he will have his hands full and will be loved forever.

Dreaming of a Black Christmas*

"I'm dreaming of a black Christmas."

"Don't be absurd, man. You know there ain't no such as a black Christmas."

"Why can't there be? Christianity originated in Africa (Alexandria). Christmas is the celebration of the coming of Christ, isn't it?"

"Yes. but still that song is about a White Christmas and the baby Jesus was white."

"The song is about a white Christmas all right, and everything else about Christmas seems to be rather white. Mary and Joseph were white, Santa Claus is white, and even them little Christmas angels are always white. That still doesn't mean I can't dream of a black Christmas."

"But a black Christmas doesn't even sound right."

"A big fat white Santa Claus coming down the chimney of a black family doesn't sound right either. A lot of things don't sound right, like an Easter bunny laying eggs. Black people got to come to their senses, man, and start doing things that make sense, not things they think look or sound right. Most of all, black people need to stop doing things because someone else is doing them."

"What's that got to do with a black Christmas?"

"It means we have got to stop making white merchants happy by going in debt for Christmas. Some black people buy so many toys and other gifts for Christmas that they don't get out of debt until the following Christmas. White merchants have a green Christmas and grin all the way to the bank. They have taken the Christ out of Christmas."

"So what can we do? We seem to be hooked now, especially our children."

---

*Originally published in the Carolinian. Used by permission.

"Are the Chinese hooked? Are Jews hooked? They have children, too, and they don't even celebrate Christmas. It's all in the way you start out."

"Are you saying we shouldn't celebrate Christmas, man?"

"Certainly not. I'm merely saying we should only do what we can afford to do for Christmas. What's wrong with one toy or one gift per child and cards to your friends and relatives? After all, merry is in the mind and Christmas is only one day a year. Having the kind of Christmas you can afford to have sounds very realistic to me."

"Me too, man...Merry black Christmas and may you have a happy black New Year."

Young, Gifted, and Black

When you're young and black, don't mean nothing.
"Hope he ain't too black."
"Check his hair."
Discrimination, limitations, degradation.
From the cradle to the grave,
Who really cares? Who loves you? Who needs you?
Black baby ... poor baby.
All da cotton dun ben picked....
All da t'bacco dun been cropped.
"Another nigger."
"Nigger ain't shit ... young or old, ridin· or walkin'."
Hard times ... little love, no love.
Learn to live wid less.
Be aware ... can't be president. Limitations.
"Why couldn't you be lighter?" Discrimination.
Love him for what?
Hide him ... can't love him. Society don't love him.
Ain't gonna be nothing. What can he be'! How can it be?
Who needs him ... 'noth er nigger?
Discrimination, limitation, degradation.

When you're gifted and black, don't mean nothing.
Think he's different, but we ain't got no money.
Didn't nobody know? Didn't nobody care?

Mama knows, but she's black, too. "Always been smart," she said.
"Nigger ain't shit," dey said
Limitations, discrimination, degradation.

Gifted, bah.

Smart, bah.

Don't know nothing ... too black ... know what?
Brain wasted . . . terrible thing to waste.
Who cares? Let 'em go. Keep 'em down.
Cure for cancer, you kidding?
Not him. Too black. Get back, for sure we'll find da cure.

Special school ... not him ... no money. Limitations.
School for gifted ... not him, outa funds, too black, anything.
Degradation.
Mechanic maybe—sounds more like it.
Something special . . . check it out. . .
Ain't gonna be nothing, told ya so.
Nigger ain't shit—gifted or no gifted.
Seen his kind. . . .

Cure for cancer, are you kidding?
Not dat nigger ... ain't smart at all ... wait 'n' see.
Discrimination.

When you're black and black, sho nuff don't mean nothing.
Get back, go back to Africa . . . anywhere.
Brought here ... taught fear ...

Second-class ... kiss ass.

Ah, my hair, why do dey care?
Lighter than me ...   my own people, you see.
Hold me back . . . back from what?

Not in da cards

Your time is up.
White is it

Nigger ain't shit.

Last hired ... first fired ... Lawd, we tired.
No God. White God. No God.
Use ours…y'all ain't got nothing.
Nigger ain't shit, 'specially a black one.

Black-black-black—you're done.
No place ...

no world ...

Can I die? ... Let me die.

Live for what?
When you're young, gifted, and black?

Discrimination, limitation, degradation.

www.ingramcontent.com/pod-product-compliance
Lightning Source LLC
LaVergne TN
LVHW091542060526
838200LV00036B/672